Charles Karel Bouley

alyson books
los angeles

MANUFACTURED IN THE UNITED STATES OF AMERICA.

THIS TRADE PAPERBACK ORIGINAL IS PUBLISHED BY ALYSON PUBLICATIONS,
P.O. BOX 4371, LOS ANGELES, CALIFORNIA 90078-4371.
DISTRIBUTION IN THE UNITED KINGDOM BY TURNAROUND PUBLISHER SERVICES LTD.,
UNIT 3, OLYMPIA TRADING ESTATE, COBURG ROAD, WOOD GREEN,
LONDON N22 6TZ ENGLAND.

FIRST EDITION: JULY 2004

04 05 06 07 08 a 10 9 8 7 6 5 4 3 2 1

ISBN 1-55583-808-1

LIBRARY OF CONGRESS CATALOGING-IN-PUBLICATION DATA
  BOULEY, CHARLES KAREL.
    YOU CAN'T SAY THAT! / CHARLES KAREL BOULEY. — 1ST ED.
      ISBN 1-55583-808-1 (PBK.)
      I. TITLE: YOU CAN NOT SAY THAT!. II. TITLE: YOU CANNOT SAY THAT!. III. TITLE.
  PN4874.B629A25 2004
    814'.6—DC22   2004046283

COVER PHOTOGRAPHY BY JOHN LIMBOCKER.

Contents

Acknowledgments

This book would not be possible without the guidance, wisdom, and inspiration of my late husband Andrew Lee Howard. He, above anyone else, encouraged me to write and always believed in that part of me. He considered it a gift I took for granted, and he was right. Well, Andrew, I no longer take it for granted. I wish you could have seen this happen because it wouldn't have existed without you. You didn't give me a voice, but you inspired it, focused it, helped it grow. I can only hope to be one tenth the writer you were. The person I am today is because I loved you and you loved me. You are my heart and the voice of reason in my head, still. I'll thank you when we meet again.

After Andrew's death there were those who kept me focused, discussed my articles with me, and inspired me with new ideas. Long before the text ever reached an editor, my dearest friend Karen Dittman would comment, criticize, critique...she and Andrew thought, and think, very much alike, and while her politics tend to drift to the right sometimes, she kept me sane enough to complete this and other projects.

Larry Flick, Sean Devereaux, Emily Johnson, Jason

Young, Daniel Amspaugh, Ken and Dennis, David Ethridge, Tommy Williams, Daniel Woltosz, Matt Seyden, and so many of my other friends who have been subjects or key players in my writing: Thanks for understanding that everything in life is a topic and that being my friend means one day you may end up in print or on the radio. You all are my family and know it, members of the "Island of Misfit Toys."

To Candy, Scott, Jake and Heather McGrath, Randy and Sandy Howard: Know that your brother, uncle, son played such an important part of this, and that your continued faith in me, sticking by me, and making me feel like family through it all means more than any words could express.

Many of these articles ran in *The Orange County Blade,* a gay and lesbian publication in California. To Bill LaPointe, the publisher, thanks for the outlet and for all the great fights about what you would and wouldn't run.

Advocate.com has been a great way for me to reach so many in the community, and I can't thank Bruce Steele enough for posting the columns, even the ones with which he disagreed. His overall help editing this book has been of great value to me, and I appreciate his wisdom, guidance, and great debates.

To Angela Brown at Alyson, thanks for taking the chance on my first actual book. What a oddity I must have seemed, coming up to sign the contracts with a photographer in tow. I look forward to working with you much more in the future. And thanks for letting me be late—I can be such a diva sometimes! Your focus and intuition about what would work took a bunch of mixed-up thoughts and made them something readable!

I am my mother's son. There are no two ways about it. And as I watched nature play the cruel trick of Alzheimer's on her, I could still see the fire, the passion, the fierce independence inside a woman who had fought adversity her entire life. Handicapped but never infirm, poor but never broken, tired but always feisty, she is the reason Karel exists, quite literally. She told me I could do anything I set my mind to, and she was right. She taught me by example that people can try to hold you down, try to classify you, try to block your path, but all that means is you've got to go around them in a different way. I could never thank her enough for simply being her. One of the greatest pains of my life was saying goodbye to her that night at Alamitos Belmont Care Facility, 305, bed 3. She left right in front of me, as well as Rebecca and Isabelle, my girls. As Oliver, Stephanie, and all the nurses gathered to say goodbye to her I realized she had touched everyone, not just me. French Fry, I hope you're finally resting; forget it, you're my mom—I hope you're running everyone crazy wherever you may be. I miss you.

I lost my father many years ago, in my 20s. He was very proud of me, of my little columns appearing in small papers. He'd carry them to the veteran's hospital with him for others there to read. Well, Dad, I'll be sure and drop a few books off there so they can see your son did it.

To David Hall and my KFI AM 640 family—Mark Austin Thomas, Rose Hernandez, Bill Handel, Stella Maroquin, Jennifer Keller, Tiffany Dennis, Michelle Kube, Anthony Smiljkovich, Phil Hendrie, Dr. Laura, Rush, Matt Drudge and so many others—thanks for the great ride and for giving me so much to talk about. And to my KGO AM 810 family— Jack Swanson, Trish Robbins, Jonathan Serviss, Christine Mathias, Gene Burns, Jason, Pam, and the crew—thanks for giving me a "second half" in such a great place.

I have had the pleasure of talking to literally hundreds of thousands of people over the years. To those that listen or read, thank you for the honor. Thank you for taking time from your life to share a little of mine. You have made my life extraordinary, filled with debate, laughter and tears, and you have allowed me to grow right before your very eyes. What a privilege it has been and continues to be.

Introduction

I've always been a writer, but I didn't always say much. I'm an entertainer, so I firs*f*t became an entertainment journalist. It's all one for me: Writing about other people's records, stage shows, movies—for publications such as *Billboard* magazine and hundreds of local gay and lesbian press outlets—was all a part of making my own "records," performing, being in the industry.

Then I started seeing things in the gay community that I had to write about, things that struck me as needing discussion. So I began writing editorials. As time progressed, the subject matter grew from just the gay and lesbian community to the world as a whole. When I started doing mainstream talk radio, everything was fair game.

But my writing, and my life, can be broken in to three very distinct periods: before Andrew, during Andrew, and after Andrew. In 1999, at Andrew's urging, I began to write editorials and not just entertainment pieces. This book is a gathering of those editorials from 1999 to 2004. Some are out of order chronologically but just seemed to flow better where they landed. The spigot Andrew helped me open doesn't seem to be shutting off, either.

I met Andrew Howard in 1989, when I was 27. We became a couple and were together 11-plus years, separated only by his death. He was a fiery redhead, in both appearance and opinion. He was a historian, political, a true part of the entire world. He was a brilliant writer who cared about what went on in foreign countries as much as his neighborhood, and even worried that the sun would extinguish in a billion years and wondered what we would do about it when it happened.

I assured him we wouldn't be here for it.

There is no doubt Andrew shaped my life and my opinions. He opened up new doors for me and made me look at things differently. His death profoundly changed me, as my writing attests.

With Andrew by my side as we arrived at KFI AM 640 in Los Angeles—the number one AM talk station in the market—my writing really took off. Our lives before that are another book entirely. So these columns and rants spring from when we opened the microphone to all of the West Coast, through the time I was forced to say goodbye to Andrew all too soon, and into my life in the years since his death. Little increments of time.

But what a time it was—and is. We were the first openly gay male couple to ever have a talk show in a major market. We had a lot of firsts. And seconds: When Andrew died, I became the second domestic partner in the state of California to file a wrongful-death lawsuit, Sharon Smith having been the first for her case against the owners of the dogs that mauled her lover, Diane Alexis Whipple, to death in San Francisco.

The journey, my journey, our journey, and my observations along the way were all chronicled in columns, editorials, and ramblings. *You Can't Say That!* is a collection of some of those. It was all a learning process for me, and I hope it will be a growing process for you, the reader, as well. Because love me or hate me, agree or disagree, someone's got to say something first before any dialogue begins. And that's what life is to me, one continuing dialogue.

Let the chatter begin.

You Can't Say That!

Americans live under the misconception that we are one of the few nations with the right to freedom of speech. Hogwash. Anyone anywhere in the world at any time can say whatever it is they wish to say—they are, in fact, *free* to say it. Here's the American fallacy: We perceive the freedom of speech granted to us by our forefathers in the First Amendment to the U.S. Constitution—"Congress shall make no law...abridging the freedom of speech, or of the press"—to mean that we have some freedom others don't. Untrue. What the forefathers were addressing wasn't the inalienable right to blather on incessantly about whatever one wishes, but what happens after it's said. In America we're supposed to have the right to speak out against our government—to speak against those things that we deem wrong and to endorse those things we see as right—and not fear repercussions from law enforcement, the government, or the private sector.

Well, guess again.

History is littered with cases of people who have in fact spoken out, only to be silenced by political or corporate pressures. Some have lost their livelihoods, others their lives, and still others have simply become outcasts, ostracized by the very community they were trying to protect through their speech.

Never was this more evident than after the tragedy of September 11, 2001. As everyone searched the debris, trying to figure out what happened and why, some began to ask tough questions: Why did this truly happen? Could it have been our foreign policy? Could those who are angry enough to fly a plane into a building actually have some ground, however shaky, on which to stand?

No one was saying what happened was justified, but many editors and columnists across the land began to ask why so much of the world had such a low opinion of the United States and if we could be, in part, to blame for this through our deeds or policies. Editors of newspapers were fired for such editorials. According to the National Coalition Against Censorship, in September 2001 Tom Gutting, city editor for the *Texas City Sun,* was fired after writing a column in which he referred to President Bush as a "scared child seeking refuge in his mother's bed after having a nightmare" for not returning to Washington, D.C., immediately after hearing about the attacks. In that same month, Dan Guthrie, a columnist for the *Grants Pass Daily Courier* in Oregon, was fired after writing a column criticizing Bush for not being more visible following the news of September 11. Bill Maher, from the TV talk show *Politically Incorrect,* wound up cancelled for his views on this and other controversial topics. Corporate America has been trying to silence filmmaker Michael Moore for years for his all-out attack on ivory towers of all kinds.

Say what you want, we're told, but you can't say *that.* One irony of the American concept of freedom of speech is the belief that everyone in our federal government supports this right. A March 19, 2003, story from ABCNews.com shows how far from true that really is. It tells of how U.S. Supreme Court justice Antonin Scalia was attending an event for the City Club in Cleveland, an event at which he was scheduled to receive an award for his unwavering support of freedom of speech. The City Club normally tapes speakers for broadcast on public television, but one of Scalia's conditions for coming and accepting the award was that no broadcast media be allowed to attend. C-Span's vice president and executive producer Terry Murphy wrote a letter to the City Club saying that the ban "begs disbelief and seems to be in conflict with the award itself. How is there free speech if there are limits to its distribution?"

Scalia made the same demand at John Carroll University, where on March 17, 2003, he gave a speech about constitutional protection of religion. He also asserted that the federal government has the power to scale back individual rights during wartime without violating the Constitution. "The Constitution just sets minimums," he told the crowd. "Most of the rights you enjoy go way beyond what the Constitution requires." There he stood, a U.S. Supreme Court justice, one of the nine ultimate guardians of the Bill of Rights, a man hailed as a leader in the fight to protect free speech—who saw nothing wrong with banning cameras and radio equipment to prevent dissemination of his views on the Constitution. There he stood, smugly warning listeners that their government had every right to shut them up, even lock them up, anytime it felt threatened.

Now, it is true that Scalia has a long-standing policy about not being recorded. But this champion of free speech takes it to the extremes. According to CNN, on April 8, 2004 Scalia was making a speech in Mississippi when Federal Deputy Marshal Melanie Rube demanded that a reporter from the Associated Press and a reporter from the *Hattiesburg American* erase their tape recordings of Scalia's comments. It's ironic that a speech about the Constitution, given in a high school auditorium in middle America, could not be recorded, and in fact, the very tapes that contained it had to be erased. It begs the question, what is Scalia so afraid of?

The contradiction between his own speech and our concept of freedom of speech is just overwhelming.

And what Scalia endorses happens all the time. In early 2003 the United States was looking at impending war with Iraq, a war many perceived as King George II's personal vendetta against the dictator Saddam Hussein. It was seen by many as a war for oil, and as a way to shift the axis of power in the resource-rich Middle East. It was also seen as a way to protect Israel—a major ally of the United States— from Saddam, a reason that many saw as vindication enough.

But not everyone was convinced, and King George had to make a plea to the American people for support. He planned to use his State of the Union address in January 2003 to do just that.

Knowing this, the Peace Action Education Fund wanted to spend $5,000 to buy six 30-second ads from the Philadelphia-based Comcast cable company, to be aired on Washington, D.C.–area feeds of CNN beginning Tuesday night, the night of the speech.

Comcast said no.

"Comcast runs advertisements from many sources representing a wide range of viewpoints, pro and con," Comcast spokesman Mitchell Schmale told the Associated Press in a statement released that week. "However, we must decline to run any spot that fails to substantiate certain claims or charges. In our view, this spot raises such questions."

Schmale's statement didn't specify what, exactly, the nation's largest cable company objected to in the commercials—what claims or charges they thought needed substantiating. The ads showed citizens exercising their freedom of speech, expressing opinions about the war with Iraq—opinions, not pie charts and graphs. Do you think Comcast has the same objection to other ads—say, those prescription drug ads that, many members of Congress allege, make false claims? Not that I've seen. Those ads are still running with zest and fervor on countless cable networks that I'd bet Comcast is happy to carry.

At a time when dissenting opinions needed to be heard in this country, the Peace Action Education Fund was told, "No, you can't say that, at least not on our airwaves." You can still buy untested diet pills, dubious exercise equipment, and magical stain removers by the truckload, without a peep about whether their "claims or charges" are substantiated. But you can't hear voices calling for peace.

Once the actual war with Iraq started—what I'd call a preemptive strike by the United States upon a oil-rich Middle Eastern nation run by a dictator the U.S. once supported, but what U.S. television labeled with tabloid taglines like TARGET: IRAQ—the often unseen war over the things you could and couldn't say really started to heat up. Ask acclaimed journalist Peter Arnett. Having won the Pultizer Prize for his coverage of King George I's 1992 Gulf War, he was fired by NBC on March 31, 2003. Why? While in Bagdad on assignment, he gave an interview to state-run TV in Iraq in which he stated the U.S. war plan had failed because of Iraq's resistance, and that they would have to draft a new plan quickly.

The corporate demand that Arnett suppress his freedom of speech came quickly, and he was pressured to apologize. On NBC's *Today* show, he said, "I said over the weekend what we all know about the war. I want to apologize to the American people for clearly making a misjudgment." His apology wasn't good enough, NBC announced the day he was fired.

Arnett said his Iraqi friends told him there was a growing sense of nationalism and resistance to what the U.S. and Britain were doing. Thinking he was protected by that "no law abridging...the freedom...of the press" clause in the Bill of Rights, Arnett failed to grasp an important corollary of the Scalia Doctrine: When we are at war, you can say whatever you want about the war, except that we're doing it wrong. If you do that, you should expect to be fired as a journalist. And if you do it on Iraqi-run TV and the interview is then picked up by Egypt's Associated Press bureau, you're out of there even faster.

Yes, Peter Arnett had freedom of speech. He was free to say it, and now he was free to do whatever he wanted without a job.

I have experienced the corporate corollary to the Scalia Doctrine firsthand. A funny instance happened while Andrew and I were at KFI AM 640 in Los Angeles. A major cell phone company was one of our sponsors—meaning, we read their ads on the air and used its service, since it had given us phones. Well, the phones just didn't work—we never had service. We might as well have been in a coal mine, for all the good those phones did us. So on our way to the station one day I threw mine out the car window. We went on the air and questioned how we could send a man to the moon but not have good cell service in a city like Los Angeles. We mentioned the company's name and that we'd be changing soon to see if anyone else was better.

The next day we had to defend ourselves to keep our jobs. The suits wanted apologies. The cell phone company wanted free ads. We were to go on the air and say we were sorry and that company had great service. We handed one of the suits our remaining phone and said no.

We kept our jobs but were admonished not to talk about any advertisers ever again. So much for freedom of speech on corporate-underwritten radio.

When Dr. Laura Schlessinger, a station mate at KFI, was embroiled in controversy over her unkind remarks about gays, hosts were encouraged not to talk about her or her controversy.

Other hosts on other stations could and did. On Dr. Laura's station, however, we were "asked" not to. There we were, the only gay male couple on radio, while Dr. Laura was in the middle of a national gay controversy, and we were "asked" not to mention it. We were reminded, in fact, that she brought in a lot more money for the station than we did. Of course, no one out-and-out prohibited us from talking about her. No one gagged us. We could have done it. We were free to do so. But the consequences were understood. Anyway, our corporate handlers pointed out, it wouldn't really be relevant to our listeners, right? What would it offer them? What new information could we bring? Why not just leave it alone?

Don't go thinking it's just the corporations and political conservatives who subscribe to variations on the Scalia Doctrine. It goes much deeper. As a gay person I was appalled, as most people were, when Matthew Shepard was killed. Andrew and I were on the air that night. I remember over the next few days reporting the details. But as the story became clear, I had problems not addressing some difficult questions. One night on the air I asked, "What was a young guy, someone small in stature, doing getting in a car with not one but two relative strangers—and straight ones at that?" He put himself in danger. He didn't deserve to die, but he didn't act very prudently about his own safety.

Well, heavens, don't say that! Many listeners were appalled—many liberal, gay listeners who wouldn't give Scalia the time of day. How dare we?

One year later, on the anniversary of Shepard's death, we put hidden microphones on a straight actor and sent him into a gay bar in Long Beach, Calif. Within 11 minutes a man offered to go home with him. The gay man brought the straight man back to a hotel room, where Andrew and I were waiting with radio microphones to question this guy: Had the death of Matthew Shepard taught him nothing about getting into cars with strangers?

We had all kinds of gay rights groups on our case over that stunt. How dare we point this out? We had spoken out against our own, exposed a frailty. No, no, no, we mustn't say that.

We're not the only ones who have found their jobs at stake for speaking our mind, of course. Most of us can't go up to our boss and tell him or her what we really think, for example, and expect to keep our jobs. In many cases that makes sense, and we acknowledge disruption and disrespect may strip us of our "freedom of speech." But in other cases, speech that's labeled disrespectful and therefore inappropriate is in fact a constructive attempt to address social problems.

Example: A teacher in Pasadena, Calif., in 2002 wrote a memo to his principal telling him that it was his observation that most of the "problem" students were black and that their behavior was a function of the different culture in which they were brought up. They had learned to behave differently in school and social situations, and the teacher suggested new teaching methods to modify that behavior. He proposed classes that were specifically designed for black students to address directly the socialization that was responsible for their disruptive habits.

He had statistics. He wanted to try and solve a problem.

Instead he was labeled a racist, came under fire from the school board, and nearly lost his job.

Did he have freedom of speech? Certainly—he wrote that memo. Was that speech really protected from repercussions? Yeah, right.

Should all speech be protected from repercussions? Or, more simply, should speech really be free? On that question, I'm torn. Sure, I like the right to print or talk about anything I want. And I don't like it when I'm censored. For example, I wrote an editorial about how most people in the gay and lesbian community get no real use out of our many gay and lesbian service centers. No one would print it. It's in this book, but the editors of my regular columns thought it went too far: I was attacking a holy shrine of the gay community, our gay centers. My freedom of speech hit a protective wall of silence. I got over it. By printing the essay here, I may even get even.

But that's the exception. For the most part I get away with a lot on radio and in print. But there is a downside to the freedom I enjoy.

Which brings us back to Matthew Shepard. I have long contended that people like Pat Robertson, Rev. Schueller, Jerry Falwell, Dr. Laura, and others whose speech reeks of hate and bigotry toward gay and lesbians—people who try to hide that hate behind the Bible—those people incite incidents like Matthew Shepard's killing, in addition to the hundreds of crimes against people of diverse lifestyles that take place all across America each day. These people spout off as fact their judgmental religious beliefs to millions of viewers and listeners and leave it to the masses to take action as they will to put that speech into action. Some resort to violence, feeling safe that the "facts" support their brutal attacks on people different from them.

Whenever such an incident is reported in the media, the orators run behind the First Amendment and demur at the idea that they told anyone to hurt anyone. Yet their speech directly affects society by serving as fertilizer for intolerance and bigotry.

That's one cost of the freedom of speech. Robertson and Falwell and most of their ilk never seem to pay the balance due on that cost. But some hate-speech orators are beginning to.

Aryan movement leader Tom Metzger, an admitted fan of my radio show, e-mailed me often. I was perplexed at the thought that someone who so obviously hated my very existence would e-mail me. Yet he was always cordial and polite and dealt with the issues at hand. But Metzger became a prime example of when society—in the form of a civil court—determines that speech has crossed the line from freedom to destruction. Metzger went to trial, even though he hadn't pulled any triggers. Prosecutors alleged that his teachings, his speech, indirectly led others to commit crimes against blacks. The civil jury awarded the family of the victims $12.5 million, to be paid as follows: WAR (White Aryan Resistance, Metzger's group) would pay $5 million; Tom Metzger, $3 million; his son John, $4 million; and two of the murderers, $500,000. Upheld on appeal on April 20, 1993, this judgment is one of the largest civil verdicts of its kind in U.S. history.

Well, why can't we sue and win millions from people like Falwell, Schlessinger, and Robertson, who openly condemn entire segments of society based on nothing more than unsubstantiated text? It's not because our detractors have God and the First Amendment on their side, as they'd like to think. It's simpler than that. Gays and lesbians aren't as far along in the movement for equality as blacks and other minorities.

When Diane Sawyer did the big Rosie O'Donnell interview in which Rosie came out, she interviewed a Florida legislator who got to go on TV and say how morally wrong homosexuality is, how it's an abomination against God, etc., etc., etc. Of course, when Jews or blacks are interviewed about causes or movements dear to themselves, never does a television or radio journalist feel the need to quote an Aryan about how inferior blacks are or why Jews don't belong here. So why do they still feel a need to give anti-gay views "equal time"? Why is it still up for debate? Clout—political and social clout, which we still don't have en masse and our enemies do. Conservatives are still free to bash away at gays and lesbians in the name of God or country. Bash a gay and it's freedom speech; bash a Jew or black, and there's a price to pay: You could lose a civil suit, lose your house, lose your job.

Just ask Sen. Trent Lott. In 2002 he spoke fondly of fellow senator Strom Thurmond's racist presidential campaign in 1948—and he soon had to step down as the Senate's majority leader. Yet for years he'd been spouting off anti-gay rhetoric with no repercussions whatsoever.

So freedom of speech really comes down to where, when, and what you say about something. Eventually that will work to our advantage, since in 100 years anti-gay views like those of the religious right will be seen as ridiculous.

But not yet.

Freedom of speech will never be absolute. Censorship will always exist, as it does now, hidden behind cute phrases like *policy* or *standards* or *ethics*. No one will ever be 100% free to speak without fear of repercussions if what they are saying is vastly unpopular or goes against the mood of the people, the government, or corporate America. Yes, we are more free than most nations, but each day we give up a little more of our freedoms, speech or otherwise, out of fear, out of a sense of "doing what's right," or out of apathy.

The Patriot Act of 2001 took away hundreds of our rights, allowing the powers that be to search homes and computers, tap phone lines, and record conversations based on nothing more than suspicion, conjecture, or innuendo, without due process and without oversight. If you're against the war in Iraq, you'd better be n careful whom you tell, or your phone may end up bugged. Arab-Americans after 9/11 have to watch what they do, or they could be detained for weeks without so much as a call to a lawyer. All of these actions our elected representatives approved, out of a desperate attempt to understand what had happened and to prevent it from happening again. And out of fear, most Americans gratefully yield up these precious rights.

Fear. Most people are afraid of truly free speech. And they should be—it's one of the most powerful rights any person, any entity, any country could have. Speech is the most powerful of all forms of communication, either live or in print. Orations have shaped history; newspaper articles can influence a nation. Think of Gandhi's words, the words of Martin

Luther King Jr., Churchill...all great orators, two of whom paid the ultimate price, their lives taken away because they exercised their freedom of speech. They were free to express themselves, and that made them targets for those who would silence them.

I can't point to a Gandhi or an MLK who's speaking out today, but there are still people out there raising the hard issues, saying unpopular things, provoking thought through words. Maybe I'm one of them, maybe I'm not. But I am grateful that today I still can have a voice. It may not be a popular one, or at times even a right one. But it's a voice nonetheless. And that's what free speech is about: giving a voice to a person, a movement, a nation.

I'll keep it up, and so should you. And if someone tells you "You can't say that," chances are not only should you keep saying it, but louder, stronger, and to more people. It's your mind—speak it. I know I do. Just be sure that when you do, you have conviction in your thoughts and words. And choose them wisely: Words are weapons, words are tools, words are power. Going against the grain is fine, so long as the goal isn't the destruction of the tree. Say what you want, and sometimes suffer the repercussions from it, but remember, speech is never free; there's always some price to pay. Just be sure you're the one paying for yours.

That's why I write about the gay community so much. You see, I'm a member of it, and how it is perceived directly affects me and my life. Being an insider, I've learned that one thing most gays and lesbians do not want is introspection. We have spent so much time being oppressed that we have become professional victims. And victims don't want to share in the blame.

Yet the only way gays and lesbians will ever move forward is to look hard and long at themselves and our community, and make some value judgments about what they see; take some responsibility for our image and actions in the world at large. The honesty that walks hand in hand with the constructive use of freedom of speech can hurt at times, if that honesty means that for once our community is forced to realize that some of what our detractors say may actually be true.

Many of my opinions and editorials that ask gays and lesbians to make such difficult judgments about themselves have made me unpopular among some in the gay community. That never was, never is, never will be my goal. Controversy for controversy's sake is something I leave to sensationalists. That's not the kind of freedom of speech I try to exercise.

I have been out since high school. I've lived more than 22 years as an out gay man. Along the way I've made plenty of mistakes, as I'm the first to admit. But I've also learned from them. And that's something I believe the community as a whole has a problem with—we don't seem to learn from our mistakes; we like to keep making them and then ask others just to deal with them. *Love us as we are, or not at all.* Well, that philosophy hasn't worked so far. For all the good that's been done, I still can't marry legally, and in more than 10 states the sex I have is illegal. I can't openly serve in the military, and in many states I can't adopt a child. Gays and lesbians are still second-class citizens.

To rise above that second-class status we must rise above ourselves. We must look at ourselves, from within, and demand more. We must be honest with each other and expect more of ourselves and our community.

Honesty—that's the one thing this book is about. My honesty, from my heart, from my life. Freedom of speech is nothing without true honesty. Can my honesty help illuminate your reality? I think so. Whatever my reality, I believe there's a shred of it in yours as well. I believe there's a common thread through all of this, gay or not—a human experience that can be shared, relevant, revealing.

I've made a career out of saying things others wouldn't.

When someone tells me "You can't say that," it's usually the first thing I'll say. I'm willing to pay the price for my freedom of speech, as long as it buys me, and my community, a higher standing in the country and the world.

Must There Be
a Great Divide?

It seemed innocent enough. Being the first openly gay couple to host a major-market drive-time radio show, and being residents of Long Beach, Calif., our desire to be part of the Long Beach Gay Pride celebration seemed like a basic no-brainer. After all, my partner Andrew and I wanted to support our community, and one way we could do that was to bring the same radio station that programs the ultraconservative talk-show hosts Rush Limbaugh and Dr. Laura Schlessinger into the Gay Pride movement by getting it to participate in the Pride parade and festival. So we arranged to appear on a station-sponsored float in the parade, and we got the station to run 60-second spots promoting the event throughout the day for free, which meant the Gay Pride message would reach a potential heterosexual audience of about 700,000 people.

It was an innocent gesture. But that's where the trouble began.

Talk radio isn't always a pleasant place. Controversy

makes ratings, and insensitivity abounds—in fact, it's almost a prerequisite. So when the ads ran during the morning drive-time show, the most coveted time on the air, the engineer dropped "taglines" under the ad, unbeknownst to anyone. The engineer, on his own, thought it would be funny to play an audible clip under the advertisement.

The taglines were "homo promo" and "butt munchers." So while the announcement about Long Beach Gay Pride was heard during the morning drive, those two taglines were heard under the ad—very subliminally but audibly nonetheless.

Anyone who listened to Bill Handel's morning show on KFI, where I was working, knew immediately this was tame for his show. He offends just about everyone: blacks, Jews, gays. He uses inflammatory phrases, including "faggot" and "faygele," to get attention, to point out the ridiculousness of it all. If they know Handel personally, as I do, they also know he is the most gay-friendly man; in fact, his support of us at KFI had been unwavering. He allowed us to fill in for him (a very big deal given our sexuality and the high ratings of his show) and rallied for us to be hired by the station full-time.

His fans knew this. Our fans knew this. But the Long Beach Lesbian and Gay Pride organization obviously didn't. When they heard of the taglines from board members who listened to the station, they "responded to an outcry from the community at the fact that a corporate sponsor of their event would allow such negativity to be presented during an ad for their event," as a letter to KFI from the Gay Pride board stated.

Well, the phone calls began. And the controversy. The promotions department at KFI, which I had asked to participate in this event, was furious with Handel's engineer and made sure everyone at the station knew they were not to have these or any other drop lines inserted around *any* promo spot, gay or otherwise. They apologized to the Pride organization over the phone.

But that wasn't enough. Soon there were board meetings at Pride, decisions to be made about our participation in the parade, three hours of phone calls by myself to Pride—the molehill of a tasteless joke had become a mountain of indignation.

The Pride organizers wanted a formal, public apology. They weren't going to get it. Handel, if he even knew about it, would only have turned it into a topic for discussion on his show—and that wouldn't be a good thing. The station takes continuous hits about Dr. Laura's show from the gay community and never responds. They love controversy. So there was no doubt in my mind this would end where it began, with the Pride organizers just as angry as ever at the station.

The Pride organizers weren't sure they wanted a KFI float in the parade, even if Andrew and I were the ones riding on it. They debated, we waited. After all, it was no skin off KFI's nose—if it wasn't for our instigation, the float wouldn't have happened. It was Andrew and me who would lose face.

As the decision by Pride to either keep us in the parade or withdraw us drew closer, I couldn't help but wonder: How is the gay community served here? Of course the remarks, the taglines, were insensitive and inappropriate. Absolutely. Were they hurtful or meant with malice? Absolutely not.

Intent is a big factor in choosing to wage war. It was shock value, not malice, that motivated the board operator to drop those lines in, and shock value that Handel wants when he uses words like "faggot." He doesn't want us killed or denied rights; on the contrary, he rallies for them. And he rallies for them to an audience that is enormous and less than 5% gay. Isn't that who should hear the cause?

Then there's us. The station made history by putting us in afternoon drive time. And it took major hits for doing so. The advertising department had to scurry to do damage control, placating good, God-fearin' advertisers that didn't want to be in a "gay" show. The politics of radio mired down everyone involved in the decision to proceed with this "grand experiment." Careers were on the line. If we as a team worked, great. If not, heads could roll, including ours.

I reminded the outraged community and its leaders to think about KFI's lineup for a moment and then judge the station's support of the gay community. Each day they presented Handel, Rush Limbaugh, Dr. Laura, consumer advocate Clark Howard. Then us. It was a complete 180 in the course of a day's programming. Two gay men were given 50,000 watts of power each afternoon to do with what we would. To show the 90% of the people who don't have to care about gay issues that we are normal people who, as one caller put it, "think and care about the same issues I do, out here driving my truck." Now, that's activism. That's support.

Then something clicked inside me. This is why our movement barely moves. This is why we as a community, and other minority communities, aren't making the headway we should. Because of the way we choose our battles. Because of the resources spent waging wars that need not be fought, because when we wage them, we lose the bigger picture.

KFI doesn't have to care about the gay community. Cold, hard fact. Gays are a very small part of their demographic. In fact, Orange County, that bastion of conservatism in Southern California between Los Angeles and San Diego, is one of their main audiences. It's no accident that they air Rush Limbaugh and Dr. Laura. The fact they even agreed to participate in Pride, much less hire us to do a daily radio show, immediately alienated a big chunk of their target audience. Yet they did it. And to show those 90% of non-supporters that KFI is supporting this cause just might change a few minds or open a few doors.

So is the greater good to alienate the station over such a small incident, one that was the result of one engineer's twisted sense of humor, one that had nothing to do with the station's commitment to us and to gay listeners, one that was forgotten by most people five seconds after it happened? Or was it so important to take them to task, however valid the grievance, and lose their support forever?

Activism is at a crossroads in all communities, and the future is perilous. In Riverside, Calif., Tyisha Miller, a young black woman, fell asleep or passed out in her aunt's car at a gas station at a well-traveled intersection. It was late at night, she'd had a long day, had a few drinks, had a flat tire, had a flat spare tire, and called some friends to come help her. She thought a man was following her, so while she waited she kept the doors locked, the music playing, and a .380 semiautomatic pistol in her lap. Then she fell asleep. Her friends arrived, tapped on the windows, and couldn't wake her up. They thought she might be foaming at the mouth, so they called 911. Police came, and within seven minutes they had broken one window.

Tyisha, startled, reached for the gun.

She was shot 12 times. Some shots hit her in the back. Four hit her in the head. She died instantly.

Rev. Al Sharpton, a professional activist from New York City, came to Riverside to launch a protest. O.J. "dream team" lawyer Johnnie Cochran took up the case against the police. Three white cops and one Hispanic were being called racist.

The real issues—of better police training—will never be addressed, because then it became a black thing thanks to Sharpton and Cochran. The white majority, who *needed* to care about this, who *needed* to rally in support of an investigation, wouldn't, because with Sharpton and Cochran involved, they simply dismissed it in their minds as another militant race thing.

The gay community often does the same thing. We alienate the 90% of the population whom we need to support us through our militant activism. We let ourselves be seen as one-dimensional: angry. We're seen as gay first—as *angry* gays—and as people second. Just by being so damned heavy and not lightening up just a bit.

Who's a better black activist, Al Sharpton or Bill Cosby? Think about it. Cosby is beloved by most of America, black or white. He's the quintessential father figure even though he's black and cheated on his wife. More nonblack Americans accept him into their homes, listen to him, and know him than they do Al Sharpton, Jesse Jackson, Martin Luther King III, or any other figure of black activism. Cosby is not a professional black man; he's not seen as one thing. And thus he does more to bring a positive image of African-Americans to the masses who need that positive image than do all the others combined.

Who's a better gay activist, Larry Kramer or Elton John? Who reaches more—who is seen as something else first, then gay? The answer is clear. While I love Larry Kramer, Elton does more to normalize gays and lesbians in the fabric of our culture.

The question is this: Why must there be a division between these two factions? Why do activists and organizations in our community, and others, seemingly want to divide instead of unite the communities they serve? There is room for all kinds of activism, as long as the goal is acceptance, equal rights, and all the others on the laundry list.

Look at our track record. We fought for gay marriage in Hawaii. Lost. Fought for gays in the military. Lost. If we don't win a few friends at the ballot box, we'll continue to lose. Self-identified gay and lesbian voters represent just 4% of those who show up at the polls, surveys have shown. That means we need another 47% of voters to be our straight allies before we can win by even a single vote. But instead of wooing those allies with our humanity, we continue to fight on our enemies' terms and follow leaders steeped in either the "in your face" activism of Stonewall or the corporate activism of the huge gay organizations that collect millions and are much ado about nothing. We get bogged down in battles that are unwinnable and won't shift into the areas where we can create the greatest change.

Case in point: As I sat arguing with the board of Long Beach Gay Pride for three hours total, and they reminded me that their event brings almost $4 million to the city of Long Beach, attracts almost 200,000 attendees, and is the greatest thing since sliced bread, I couldn't help but remember a friend who moved here 12 months ago and needed to transfer from AIDS Services Orange County to the Center Long Beach's AIDS program. He was turned away because they didn't have the funding to hire another caseworker to handle new cases. If Long Beach Gay Pride is so great, I wanted to say, if so much money is being generated and if the board has so much time that they can sit and talk to me for three hours about a "buttmuncher" tagline, why can't they solve the problem of hiring one new AIDS caseworker? I'm told it would take $60,000 per year to support one. If the Pride board brings $4 million to Long Beach, how about finding a way to funnel $60,000 of that to the center? Or even just spending three hours in a meeting that would help change something instead of three hours with me on the phone?

I don't understand. Andrew and I were criticized for not taking our station to task over this. Yet the station stands behind us, supports us, employs us, goes to our events (they were involved in an AIDS walk that year as well), and allowed us to be who we were every day to a huge community that needs to hear such things. Yet somehow we were the bad guys for not taking them to task.

The bad guys. As I sat and stared gratefully at the three-page story on Andrew and me in *The Advocate*, the national gay newsmagazine, I remembered how two years earlier, when I had a major recording deal with Jellybean Benitez, that magazine wouldn't cover me because "gay-friendly or gay music acts are a dime a dozen." Funny, there were no other openly gay acts on Jellybean's label. As the *Los Angeles Times* did a three-page Calendar section piece on us, I laughed that *none* of the major L.A. gay press (*Edge,*

Frontiers, David, Gay and Lesbian Times) had even called Andrew and me for an interview. Our first local coverage was to be the cover of the Orange County Blade, a gay publication that serves Orange County and Long Beach. As we were booked at huge events like the Long Beach Grand Prix, The First Annual Women's Fair at the L.A. Convention Center, the Hula Festival at Long Beach Harbor (all allegedly heterosexual events), I wondered why the one gay event brought us so much trouble.

The fact is that the community leadership didn't support us because we weren't the activists they wanted. We didn't sit on the radio every day for three hours preaching about gay causes. That would have turned off our listeners—including most of the gay ones, believe me. Gay and straight, they would have all tuned out. And keeping our 90% straight audience tuned in and learning to be tolerant of us through association was the key. *Making* them care about us, and interjecting a few things they should know along the way.

I called Andrew "my husband" on the air, in drive time. When we talked about cheating spouses, for example, we'd talk about how we'd feel if either of us ever cheated on the other. Two gay lovers talking about their relationship, on the radio, in drive time. When we did stories on the government's using polygraph tests for job hirings, I underwent one on the air and was asked if I'd ever cheated on Andrew (no), and which of our two dogs I loved more (I confessed that it was our new one, Ally), or if I really liked Andrew's mom, my mother-in-law (I do). When we did the commercial for Ortho Mattress, we said, "We sleep on an Ortho, our bed is an Ortho." Two gay lovers talking about sleeping together, on the radio, in drive time in L.A. Call me crazy, but I think that does more for advancing gay rights than demanding an apology letter or picketing some organization.

There is a forest and there are trees. Let's not lose sight of the forest while busily trying to chop down meaningless trees. Leaders, please recognize that you deserve equality not because you are gay but because you are human. Be seen as human first, gay second. Stop fighting those who help you, even if they still offend you on some levels. Learn that no ally is perfect and that you can change that ally from within more than from without. Learn checkbook politics. Act normally and be treated the same. Act separately and be treated as such.

When all was said and done, Andrew and I had such a bad taste in our mouths that he didn't want to ride in the parade. So I rode on a float with Momma (a local drag diva) while KFI had its van with the KFI lettering a few floats behind. I was also scheduled to introduce people on the main stage that afternoon. After the parade I had a fever that spiked at 104 degrees. I tried to call and cancel but couldn't reach anyone. They thought I canceled for political reasons, when I was at home sweating like white trash writing a check for the light bill. To date I have never been asked back to do anything for Long Beach Gay Pride, even though I remain one of the most visible gay residents of Long Beach.

The View From Santee

Monday, March 6, 2001, 10:10 a.m.

I knew the minute I heard on CNN: "Breaking news in Santee, Calif., a town right outside of San Diego, where a lone gunman has shot classmates, leaving 13 wounded and two dead..." I knew that minute that we should pack an overnight bag. Breaking news in our area means we're going to be there. It's part of what our talk-radio show—*Karel & Andrew Live*—is all about. We see things firsthand so we don't just talk about them, we experience them. That's why we went to Florida to cover the custody battle over Cuban boy Elian Gonzalez and why we have to be out in the world in general.

Then the madness begins: Call our producer. Get directions. Start lining up interviews. Where are the meetings of those affected going to be? Where now are the kids from the school where the shooting occurred? Where are their parents? Does the MiniDisc Recorder have a full battery charge? Does the car have gas? Do I have any blank discs for recording audio on hand? Is there a KFI reporter in Santee already who can give us a heads-up? Where will we stay? Who will feed our dogs? Is there a place to broadcast? Did I have an appointment with Mom for lunch today? Who will edit the audio from the scene? Does Andrew need to cancel his script meeting? Each question answered within minutes, first addressed on a land line and then on a cell phone as Andrew and I throw the essentials into the car and jet out the door.

On the way down to this small community a couple hours south of Long Beach where we live, I have more conversations with our producer while Andrew scans the radio for updated news reports. He's also reading a book on how to build a chicken coop. Off to a murder scene but forever informed about the backyard. You gotta love him!

The trip is a familiar one. San Diego is a beautiful city, a perfect ride by train. San Diego is a nice gateway to the rowdy Tijuana, and it's a city rich in good food and good fun. But not today. Today, when we park the car, we'll be feet away from where another urban tragedy has occurred.

We veer off the familiar Interstate 5 onto the smaller Highway 52. While approaching Santee, I can't wonder out loud about the geography of this crime. Isn't this sleepy community, nestled in a valley 15 minutes away from a busy metropolis, the very place you go so this *doesn't* happen?

Andrew disagrees. "This is just the place that breeds this kind of behavior," he comments. "Look, that store right there says it all: GUNS AND LIQUOR."

Hard to argue with that logic, but yet I remain optimistic about the community. I am quite sure it is just a group of working-class citizens who want a small-town feel close to a metropolitan area like San Diego. They didn't breed a 15-year-old who could go to school carelessly to go wound 13 people and then kill two, did they?

As we travel down Mast Avenue from the freeway, our senses are heightened. We see orange cones and people blocking a driveway to what appears to be a school. The flag is at half-mast. Is this the place? Where are the satellite trucks the networks use for live shots, with their enormous satellite dish uplinks or 40-foot-tall radio antennas? No, this isn't Santana High School, it's another school in Santee. And it is on lockdown. Parents are driving there in droves to pick up their children. No one is getting in or out who doesn't belong there. So where is Santana High? We know to look up to the sky. We do, and see six helicopters hovering over an area about a half mile away. If that doesn't mark the spot, then the Pope is also in Santee today.

While driving, the city looks fair enough—not excessively wealthy but very Buena Park, Calif. It appears to be a mixture of the upper working class and lower-to-average middle class. We pull into the strip mall across the street from another mini mall, across the street from the high school where the shootings occurred. Police had barricaded Mast Avenue, so most of the traffic in the area is media and family. When we get out of the car we see the circus that these crime scenes become: at least 20 national and local television news vans and trucks, reporters set up for live shots, perfectly made-up faces with soft lighting emanating from the top of a video camera. There are producers on cell phones, hundreds of them, calling in details, finding the next shot, the next angle, the next part of the story. The print media can be seen with small recorders in their hands and tablets of yellow paper or spiral notebooks clutched tightly. Radio reporters are also milling about, with microphones emblazoned with their station's name (in case they get in a camera shot) attached to cassette or MiniDisc recorders. And then there's us, two talk show hosts. The only radio talk-show hosts who I've ever run into at these scenes. Two gay guys who host a show. One with a microphone, one with a backpack in which is nestled Martha Stewart's guide to the backyard, just in case there's some time for reading.

Perhaps the lack of radio talk-show hosts at these scenes is why I always feel a little uncomfortable. Because we're not news reporters. We deal with news in a different way, in an interpretive way. News reporters are stuck with facts and provide an unbiased opinion of the world (in theory). We get to be as biased, compassionate, jaded, or unconventional as we wish. That's our job. But Andrew and I have to do more than sound off. We have to understand the news, put a face on it. And more times than not, that effort has changed our view completely on so many issues.

I grab the recorder and microphone with its bright orange mike flag and put on our official LAPD Press ID, the wonder badge that tells the police we're approved to be behind the lines. Without the luxury of a producer—the guy or gal in a news team who usually does most of the prep work and scheduling—the job of getting interviews falls to Andrew and me. We know the facts: Fifteen-year-old Charles Andrew Williams took his father's .22 revolver to school and shot 15 people, killing two. He had told people beforehand that he was going to do it. No one went to the authorities.

Those were the facts. Now it's time for the feelings.

I always feel like an invader when walking up to a victim or someone shaken by tragedy. That's why I go out of my way to make sure they want to speak to me at that moment. It's idealistic, I know. But Andrew and I feel strongly about not letting our job rob us of our basic humanity. There are some things you don't do for a story, and at the top of that list is cause more pain to someone already in pain.

Soon people do agree to talk with me. As always, as I meet one person, he or she tells me of another, and so on, and soon the interviews begin. While I'm out doing interviews, Andrew mans the cell phone. A difficult task. The town probably has one cell site, and right now its nerves are worked. Getting a call out would be easier on Mt. Everest. He also listens and watches. Observes. Andrew usually remembers more and sees more than me by *not* being in the exact middle of it. He sits at the nearby Del Taco and listens to conversations, hoping to hear anything that will help us present a fair story tonight to our listeners. He mingles with the press, walks around the shopping center.

My first interview is with a 14-year-old named Andrew C. As we stand outside the Albertsons grocery story and Round Table Pizza in Santee, near the corner of Magnolia and Carefree avenues, he tells me how his friend just pointed a gun at his head in the men's room.

"Not five feet away from my head...I just stood there," he recalls. Andrew C. is just looking forward at me, very matter-of-fact, yet in a daze of sorts. His eyes are glossed, and he has a look on his face that a 14-year-old shouldn't have.

"I didn't know what to do. The school hasn't covered this kind of stuff. Then he ran out the door. I ran out and saw that the 'narc' was already shot. I stood there, not believing this. This guy I knew, Andrew, was shooting people. I ran. I ran. I wanted out of there."

Next interview: Andrew C.'s father. He is a man deeply troubled by the event, and equally as troubled that every major news network has called his house even though he has an unlisted number. Little does he know that, in the days of Internet reverse phone books and people-search functions, privacy is over. There are people on-staff at most media outlets whose sole purpose in life is to find hard-to-find people.

"I moved away from New York years ago with my family to get away from this very thing," he states, watching his son as more cameras move around him.

"Do you want to stay?" I ask.

"Right now I'm not so sure..." His voice trails off as he walks over to pull his son away from the eyes of the world.

Next is Stephanie, a girl who knows the shooter. She stands staring at the football field, black slacks, white poly-ester shirt half unbuttoned, jet-black hair, with piercings in her ears, eyebrows, and lip.

"Andy was an outcast. People picked on him for trying to fit in too hard and for being too skinny," she says.

"Yes, but I can tell that you've had your share of comments made about your appearance, and I certainly have been the victim of ridicule, and we didn't kill anybody," I say.

"I guess he just took it to heart. Kids can be cruel." She stares at the helicopter above.

As the day wears on, the scene thins. Parents and children have been reunited. Witnesses are still being interviewed in the Orthodox church located right across from the shopping plaza near the school. Kids still want to talk, but not kids who saw anything, just those looking for 15 minutes of fame. Andrew overhears three kids turn down an interview in the Del Taco. In their words, they will only do "live network television, no rinky-dink news agencies."

The crews break down the equipment and rush to the city hall for a 2 P.M. press conference. Then they have to get back here for the 5 o'clock live shot for local news. I find Andrew and figure it's time to leave. On the way back to the car I see a young girl with her parents, leaving the Orthodox church. She's holding a teddy bear given to her inside, obviously. She's a witness. It's my job to go talk to her. I ask Andrew to go the car and put our stuff away, and tell him I'll be right back. I walk over and talk to this girl, just another kid trying to make sense of it all.

"Picture this," Heather begins. "I hear the shootings. I seen Andy come around the corner with a gun. Some people are on the ground. I ran so fast. I was there about 2.5 seconds. I get 20 feet and start having an asthma attack. I run to a house right across the street and use the phone. I call my mom, tell her there's been a shooting, beg her to come quickly, all while not being able to breathe. On top of that, it was the [answering] machine, so I had to call back," she continues, clutching her teddy bear with one hand and twisting her hair with the other.

"Then, after she [came and] got me, I had to come back. I had to be here with my friends, the people who witnessed this. We share something now," she concludes.

"This town is full of unsupervised kids," her mother adds. "We're not dirt-poor, but really wealthy people wouldn't live here, if you know what I mean. And sometimes that part of the town comes out. Like today..." she concludes, grabbing her daughter and husband and hurrying to their car.

Andrew and I get in the car. I tell him I think I've gotten some good audio, but I'm not sure. There was so much going on, so many stories, mixed with a few tears. Reality hits and I realize we need a place to edit this. I check our messages and find out that our travel editor, Andrea Rademan, has arranged a room for us at the famous Hotel Del Coronado on Coronado Island near San Diego. It's one of the nicest hotels in the area—they filmed *Some Like It Hot* there—and I get to see it because two kids died. It doesn't seem right. Of course, no time for the guilt. The accommodations are flawless, the ocean stormy and beautiful, and I have 45 minutes of audio to dump into my PowerBook, upload to the station, and edit in less than two hours.

As I begin to record the audio into the computer, Andrew and I listen. We know not to discuss too much about it before the show so that we're passionate and original on the air. But we sit and wonder: Why? How could this happen again? No metal detectors? Gun control? Economic factors? Bad seed? Bad parenting? All of the above? And what should happen to the shooter, Andy Williams? Should he be tried as an adult?

As the audio uploads, we pack up our headphones and head out to KOGO San Diego. They're letting us in for the evening to broadcast. The show opens and the debate begins. We're on 7 to 9 P.M. now, and we spend the entire time on this topic. After the red light finally goes off, a fiery two-hour show is over, along with the day. Andrew and I are still arguing, disagreeing on the philosophy behind the event. We open the door to the studio and there's a banner: SAN DIEGO LOVES KAREL AND ANDREW. We ask how it got there, and the engineer tells us some fans brought it by. Very touched, we pick it up and head to the car.

We order room service on our way back to the hotel, from the menu we took with us. Tonight we get to do one of our favorite things in the world, order room service and watch a Hollywood hit on pay-per-view. A storm is brewing as we eat, and the palms rustle as the ocean churns. We look around our room and realize that tonight there are two families turning out the lights in rooms where their teenagers just last night were asleep.

Why? Don't ask. Because we Americans don't want to hear the real answers.

Schools, as they exist, don't work. Test scores reveal a majority of schools are nothing more than day care, and not very good day care at that. Would you give your child over to a day care agency that has lost more than 20 kids to gun deaths in the past two years? The public school system has, and it is full. Why do we allow 500 or more hormonal, testosterone-filled teens to gather in the same place every day? Across the country malls are outlawing groups of five or more teens after 6 P.M. because of the associated dangers of letting teens congregate. Why don't we make grade schools larger, when kids are younger and easier to handle sociologically, and make high schools drastically smaller, more manageable, where counselors and teachers can take the time to find the abused, the picked-on, those who need special attention before they grab a gun?

And what about the gun issue? After doing some homework I found that in the past two years more teenagers have died of gunfire in this country than in the past 50 years in all European nations with gun control.

How far would Andrew Williams have gotten with a baseball bat?

charles karel bouley

"Yes, but if someone wants one, they could always get one." Granted, serious criminals will always be able to get weapons they need. But Williams wasn't a serious criminal until he found his father's gun. Most shooters aren't "serious" criminals until they shoot—and make no mistake, they shoot because they can.

How could the community not respond to Williams's threats? In a post-Columbine era, who really knows what to take seriously and what not to? So many officials have over-reacted in such cases that many are hesitant to come forward and take action.

No one thought he'd actually do it. Well, he did. Now what?

Should Williams be tried as an adult? We don't want to hear that our criminal justice system is not about rehabilitation but incarceration. We'd like to think of ourselves as a compassionate society trying to fix criminals' broken minds. But we're not. Out of sight is truly out of mind. So, since we don't want to rehabilitate this 15-year-old, why have a pretense of it? He *is* an adult. He became one when he picked up the gun.

Today's teenagers are adults. We sexualize them by 12 or 13, earlier if you're the Ramseys of Colorado. Young girls are entering puberty and starting their periods on average of four years earlier than their grandmothers and two to three years earlier than their mothers. By the time a child is 15 today he or she has been exposed to more news, information, imagery (violent and otherwise) than any 20-year-old of the previous generation. It's a different world, and we have different youth. We schedule them, like ourselves. We organize them. Cell phone them. Palm Pilot them. Ask them to get involved in national politics. Let them drive our marketing, our media programming, our world. Hell, at times it *is* their world. Are they adults? Of course they are. Eighteen or 21 is no longer when children "come of age." Among many kids today, 18 or 21 is midlife. Soon 16-year-olds will be getting apartments to be closer to school.

We did this. We changed it, those of us over age 30. We

changed the world, and the rules, and now we're scratching our heads and wondering how it got this way. But we really know how.

We could be philosophical. We could say violence is natural. After all, our country was established through violence against our own people in England, and violence against the natives who lived here before us. We were established in war and have been fighting ever since. We love violence. It shocks us. It appalls us. It created us.

What can we do to make sure an event like the Santee shooting doesn't happen again? Plenty. But we don't want to. We don't want to deconstruct and reconstruct the little-red-schoolhouse theory of education that we like to think has been tried-and-true for 200 years. We don't want gun-control laws that work, that may step on our God-given right to blow away someone with a 9mm. We don't want to voluntarily police our entertainment media. We don't want to admit that young white men don't handle social situations well, tend to be racist, and have a propensity for violence—because we'd be admitting too much about ourselves as adults. And we certainly don't want to admit that it's our historical right to pick on the weak and point out the flaws of others to divert attention from ourselves.

Today the news crews have moved on. So have Andrew and I. But we leave Santee changed a little, optimistic that an open dialogue about this will in some way change an outcome someplace else. We sit down to watch a mindless film to take our minds away. Great. *Carrie* by Brian De Palma. You know the story: A young girl who's picked on by everyone at school and comes from a dysfunctional family kills most of her schoolmates in the gym.

You mean this concept isn't new? A 25-year-old film touched upon it then? School rage and revenge? What a relief. I thought it was just the 21st century that seemed so god-awful.

Spinning Their
Wheels With Flair

Today at the hallowed gates of Paramount Pictures in Hollywood, yet another protest against radio entertainer Dr. Laura Schlessinger took place. The event was organized by well-intentioned but misguided gay activists hell-bent on stopping Paramount from airing Dr. Laura's new syndicated TV talk show. What all the protesters seem to be missing is that they're helping Dr. Laura far more than they could ever hurt her—and that in and of itself is counterproductive.

Of course, working at the same station as Dr. Laura and being a gay couple, Andrew and I shared many of the objections about Laura that the protesters were voicing. We were presented with a great dilemma: How could we not go on the air each day and spend a majority of our time denouncing Dr. Laura's comments, which aired only one hour before our show? The answer was obvious. Most of the time, we could ignore her, because talking endlessly about her would only validate her, give her credibility, and raise her public image (good or bad) to an even higher level. Why buy into that? Let her hire her own publicist. Besides, there was an unspoken rule at KFI about *not* discussing Dr. Laura, precisely because her show brought so much revenue into the station.

Here are the facts. Dr. Laura Schlessinger is not a psychiatrist or psychotherapist. She's a radio entertainer. To get far in this business takes publicity and controversy. Fifteen million–plus people tune in to her each day to hear what she has to say and ask her for advice. If you don't like what she has to say, turn her off. And if you're dumb enough to let what she has to say affect your life, seek a real therapist. But the fact is, not only does she have the right to say what she does (under the First Amendment), she also feels (or claims to) that she has the biblical foundation and moral conviction to say it. And she gets paid very well to do it. Why? Because love her or hate her, people listen. In fact, in radio, the more a host is hated, the more those who hate them listen. Odd but true.

The activists marching outside Paramount say she is full of hatred, that her words inspire incidents like the murder of Matthew Shepard. They contend that if her remarks were anti-Semitic or anti-black, she'd be shut down without a moment's notice. All that may be true; and if so, why promote her? That's what the Web site StopDrLaura.com, the protests, the proclamations do. Promote her. When the evening news flashes the stories, whose picture is shown? The activists'? Of course not. Dr. Laura's. Paramount couldn't *buy* this much publicity for her. Every time a gay person gets on the air and denounces her, anyone who agrees with her tunes in and those who have never heard of her watch or listen to see what it's all about. And that increases ratings. And that spells success.

So what to do about the problem that is Dr. Laura? There is no doubt she is ill-informed about the gay and lesbian community and hides behind a veil of bigotry. Obviously, Paramount should drop her show, right? Wrong. They knew what they were buying when they optioned it. Asking her to change is wrong. It would be like asking Rush Limbaugh to embrace liberal politics. Don't try to make an apple an orange. Groups like GLAAD (Gay and Lesbian Alliance Against Defamation) that met with Paramount with a list of demands or concerns about Dr. Laura should be referred again to the First Amendment, or to the court system.

So we should get a group of celebrities together, protest her, and spend thousands on ads in *Variety* and other newspapers denouncing Dr. Laura, her views, and Paramount—right? Wrong. I'm sure Dr. Laura appreciates the free advertising, as does Paramount. And as for celebrity protests, does anyone really pay attention to that sort of thing anymore? Oh, another group of gays with some liberal celebrities are protesting some right-wing bigot. That's refreshing and new. And such a great allocation of limited resources. The gay community doesn't have an unlimited budget to fight battles, and truth be told, they misappropriate their funds on these kinds of newspaper ads and insignificant protests.

So where does that leave the anti–Dr. Laura movement. Right where it started: nowhere. Where should it be going? Simply put, to the pocketbook. Dr. Laura is Dr. Laura because she is a commercially viable entity. Millions of dollars are made on her show. Hit her where it counts, in the pocketbook. Organize well-thought-out and well-backed boycotts and negative publicity campaigns against her advertisers. Take out full-page ads denouncing them, and name names. As soon as she's seen as noncommercially viable, she's gone. Remember, it's never about the viewpoints, it's about the money.

More importantly, how about countering Dr. Laura with support for shows that present an opposing viewpoint? Why not use the thousands being spent and call upon the gay elite of the entertainment industry to create programming that presents a more balanced view of not only gay issues but of a more tolerant world in general? Where are the gay networks? Five hundred cable channels and not one gay-and-lesbian themed? Four major talk-radio stations in the Southern

California market alone, and only two with openly gay hosts, and none with financial backing or even major support from the same protesters out in the streets denouncing the good doctor. Hundreds of thousands being spent on newsprint advertising denouncing Dr. Laura and hardly a penny spent on promoting anything positive about the community itself, or anyone in it of note.

Andrew and I entered the firestorm of talk radio on KFI every day, one hour after Dr. Laura. We suffered our share of hate mail and bigotry. One day KFI moved our time slot from 4–7 P.M. to 7–10 P.M., out of the coveted "drive time" slot. I received more than 3,000 e-mails from nongay parents, fathers, mothers, children, all expressing how much they'd come to love and support the show.

Why do I bring this up? Because that's how this battle is won. Incorporate, don't segregate. Normalize the community and those who oppose it will seem ridiculous. Give Dr. Laura the rope to hang herself by providing positive role models, allocate funds to actually support those doing the good, and stop spending so much time fighting unwinnable battles. Even if Paramount caves, Dr. Laura will be heard. Her radio show is stronger than ever and her new book will be a best-seller. How about creating a counter-hero to balance the scale? How about throwing support behind someone, something, some entity that can equal the playing field? It may not be as glamorous as carrying a sign, getting some celebs together, or getting 7 million hits on a Web site, but it's hell of a lot more effective.

•

Now it's a couple of years later and Dr. Laura is gone. The gay activists think they've won a battle. But they didn't really. Was it them, or just the fact that her show was bad? A mixture of both, and more of the latter. She didn't perform in the ratings, she has a face for radio, as they say, and wasn't personable enough to pull off television. Like many talk show hosts before her who tried to make the transition, she could not.

Yes, advertisers pulled out. And that is a testament to the gay movement. But dollar for dollar spent, not really a wise investment. Trust me, if the show had been a hit, they would have quietly come back on. And more importantly, Laura still has her voice, and her millions. And now those protesters have moved on to another battle when the previous war was never really won. She's still out there, saying whatever she wants, to even more people than on television. And still no counter-hero. No talk show supported, funded, or created for or by gays in a major market. Laura still collects her check while GLAAD pats on the back the producers of *Will & Grace* or *Queer as Folk,* and protesters now gather to extol the evils of eating Chilean sea bass.

are very funny. An inroad made. But it doesn't matter. Another quote from me is used to denounce KPFK's gay-themed shows *IMRU* and *This Way Out,* two shows I not only support but also admire for their tenacity and longevity. Misquoted? No, just not fully quoted. I simply said they do a good job but don't do much to progress our movement because they preach to the masses.

Then comes Al Rantel, a conservative, sometime apparently self-loathing gay male on KABC, a competing L.A. station. The few times I've heard him, he's seemed to downplay his sexuality. Here he is again, saying things about Andrew and me such as "They won't last because the gimmicks and novelty of a gay couple won't baffle people for long." He's made other derogatory statements about us that I've laughed off. But you have to wonder why he says these things. Shouldn't he be proud of us? We don't compete with him. I was proud of him before I saw his true colors. Now I'm ashamed of him. Yet I've never spoken negatively of him in public. Even in the article that he's being quoted in, there's no negativity from me about him.

Where do his comments come from? Is he jealous because he's on a 5,000-watt station and ours is 50,000 watts? Is he upset that KFI didn't hire him a year ago and he had to go to a lower-ranked talk station? Is he mad that we don't do gay topics? Does it bother him that his show is on from noon to 3 P.M. and we're on from 4 to 7, one of the most coveted spots on radio? So many questions and no answers, only negativity. And words like "gimmicks" and "novelty" used to describe a 10-year committed relationship such as ours...how long has he maintained a solid relationship? Andrew and I have battled adversity, life-threatening illness, and bigotry, and done it all without denying our sexuality. Our topics are relevant, some exclusive and groundbreaking. Where's Al? Yakking about prison rape, the reason nelly men are worse than masculine men, and chatting with the author of the week. That's fine for him. Who am I to tell him what to do? But while doing it, perhaps he should reconsider condemning two members of his own community who are working hard to change minds while just trying to do their jobs.

And as for *Frontiers*—what kind of integrity does it show that in an article about the inroads we've made at radio as a whole it prints such negative comments not just by Rantel about us but as its entire slant? The "inroads" article seems more about bitching than about the great things so many gays and lesbians are doing in radio across the country. Yes, even Rantel, because while I'm not fond of him, at least he's working, presenting an example of being (somewhat) out.

So I sit back and realize that it's a fight on all levels.

Why bother? Simple. Here's an excerpt from an e-mail I received three days ago. It literally made me cry:

Hi, guys. The very first day you started on KFI I was preparing dinner with my mouth wide open and eyes bugged out. What was I hearing? Two men who were gay on a popular and favorite radio show! OH MY GOD! Should I laugh or cry? What do I, a married woman in her 40s, have in common with two young gay men? NOTHING!

When my husband walked in the door from work he wanted to know who the hell was on the radio? I told him that these two guys were John and Ken's replacement. WHAT?? TWO GAY GUYS?? WHAT IS THIS STATION THINKING?? OH MY GOD!

For the most part I didn't tune in to KFI during your time slot, but every now and then I would quickly tune it on just to hear what topics you were talking about. When I did this I found myself listening closely to what you had to say. I was shocked! I found that YOU believed in what I believed with most issues. HOW COULD THIS BE?? How could I have the same views as YOU when it came to gun control, child rearing, etc. YOU were gay...you couldn't have the same views as ME!

Then the real test came. Three times this summer my husband and I drove to Las Vegas. Guess what station comes in perfectly clear for the whole trip? It just happened that during our trips out and back you were on.

At first my husband said that there was NO WAY he was listening to your show, but on our first trip back there was BIG NEWS. It was the day the crazy in Atlanta was shooting fellow investors and family. We listened to your show and my husband said, "OH MY GOD...I agree totally with these guys!" I did also. Hmmmmmm...what was happening to us?

By our third trip we tuned in to you as if we were old friends. My husband was shocked that your views on most things were the same as his, and I was MORE than shocked that I also agreed with your views. OH MY GOD! BTW, on our third trip back to Orange County from Vegas Andrew was covering the fire. We loved this because we were driving through smoke on I-15.

Now you are a part of our afternoon. We laugh AT your jokes not AT your lifestyle, we listen to your interviews with an open mind, we respect your commitment to each other. In other words, you have opened our minds and taught us that we truly are all the same, regardless of lifestyles. Ignorance is not bliss, it is hateful. Thank you both for leading us on one of life's learning journeys.

You know, forget about Rantel, *Frontiers*, and all the other battles. Notes like that are reason enough to take it all. Phew. There, an exhale.

American First, Hyphenate Second

Americans are the victims of a hate crime—and they don't like it. The suicide pilots who plunged into the World Trade Center towers and the Pentagon perpetrated one of the worst hate crimes the world has ever seen. Americans found it hard to believe that anyone could hate so much that they would simply attack someone because of their nationality, their beliefs.

Some of us could imagine it. I'm a member of a group in which it is commonplace to be or to know a victim of an unprovoked attack borne out of such hate. Every week there's some assault or murder in my community—some subtle, some involving fence posts in Wyoming.

It doesn't feel good, does it Middle America? Most unprovoked and irrational attacks don't. And in the shock and grief to follow the attacks, something has happened, if only fleeting, some miracle of miracles. The shocking event is that a majority of Americans have started getting it right. We finally understand. We are Americans first and foremost—not Afro-

Americans, not Gay Americans, not Italo-Americans or Muslim-Americans, not Latin Americans...we are Americans above all else.

The press dubbed it a unification of America. I've watched it become an all-out miracle. Suddenly, it doesn't matter where you stand politically, morally, socially, sexually. All that matters is that you are an American and you and your loved ones could be under attack or could have been killed.

The unification was so strong, not even the Good Reverend Falwell could make a blip on the social radar when he pronounced gays, the ACLU, feminists, and abortionists partially to blame for the attack. He sounded preposterous to even the most red of necks. We Americans know who the enemy is, and right now it isn't the queer next door or the lady down the street who opted out of a pregnancy. The enemy for this new war is not one person, but terror, evil, hatred. A pretty broad and ingrained enemy indeed.

Our president's intention to seek out "evildoers" is a noble one. I'm there. But as we Americans proceed in this battle, we're going to have to make some hard decisions and difficult observations about we the people. We need to make sure the brushstroke against terror and hatred is wide enough to include the land between our own borders.

Evildoers, terrorists, and hatemongers are all faceless entities. They are people motivated by feelings and emotions rooted in complex and multifaceted social and cultural influences. And they are people who don't have to come from a country ending in *stan*.

It is not possible to annihilate entirely those who hate. And strictly logistically, where do we stop? The Irish Republican Army is a hate group. A terrorist cell. Do we let it exist because it doesn't affect us? Haven't we declared war on terror and hatred worldwide?

The battle lines must include the land between the Pacific

and Atlantic oceans, because as our patriotism and unification begins to fade and as the war drudges on, we must remember that we are a changed people. Tragedy and loss forever change a person's very fabric—and some of those changes should be for the better. Perhaps this can wake the logic and reason in all Americans.

Let's remember that right here in the United States we have groups that would seek to overthrow our government and that have arsenals with which to do it. Will the war on terror, the war on hatred include fighting them? And let's remember that we still live in a time where, right here, right now, men get beaten and left to die tied to fence posts or dragged behind pickup trucks because they live a lifestyle other than the majority's or are a color still thought a minority. How about realizing the ridiculousness of that hatred and realizing we are Americans first? We have a bond now.

It won't be easy, but the events surrounding the attack on America prove it can be done. We ourselves have a bloody or vindictive past. Doctors have been killed for performing legal medical practices; hatred is broadcast daily under the guise of religion; drug addicts rot in jail for their own addictions; color not only divides but kills; and presidents get crucified for blow jobs.

Conflict is in our social fabric, no doubt. Perhaps these events will slow the fever pitch at which so much unnecessary violence or evil has been going on in the recent past. Think about the weeks before the terrorist attack. The biggest thing was Connie Chung talking to a no-account elected official about whether he slept with a missing girl. The Justice Department interviewed this guy, and so did every major law enforcement division of government. The news media was transfixed. And all the while terrorists were living here, watching the public destruction of a marriage and career while planning their own very public destruction. Resources wasted? History will be the judge.

Perspective is what changed on September 11, 2001—a gaining of national perspective. It became clear that most things we thought were important pale by comparison with tragedy of such proportion. The focus shifted from how we are different—Republican, Democrat, conservative, liberal, religious, agnostic, black, white, brown, yellow, homosexual, heterosexual—to the fact that we all have one thing in common: America.

As we progress let's learn to strip the tags we put before that word, American. No longer is anyone something else first and then American. The order has shifted, the hyphens removed. And if that thought should remain, then suddenly none are that different and we truly become a cohesive one.

Unimaginable? So was collapsing the World Trade Center. Stranger things have happened.

Time to Turn in My Toaster Oven

I am a 39-year-old child, seeing everything through brand-new eyes—at least when it comes to single-gay-male life. I haven't done the "single" thing very much. In the late '70s and early '80s I was in a four-year relationship—in high school and college, no less. When that ended, four months later I found myself in another relationship, which lasted eight years. Four months after that one ended, I met my first real lover, and we were together nearly 12 years, separated only by his death. So now here I sit, a single gay male in the new millennium. And it is far more dismal than even I had envisioned. It's enough to make me want to turn in my toaster oven.

It's been a revealing time, this past year of singlehood. For instance, I have realized I owe the producers of the show *Queer as Folk* an apology. You see, when it first came on I publicly begged heterosexuals not to watch it. The shallow, sex-obsessed drug addicts didn't represent the entire gay community, and I didn't want nongays to get the idea in their heads that we are that horrible stereotype. Well, I was wrong. We are that horrible stereotype. Not only do we embody it, we embrace it. We reward it. We fight for the right to be it.

Disagree? Get over it. And while I hate to burst your bubble, it gets worse. How? Well, because we know better and still choose to be everything our critics claim we are. Bars are still full of substance-abusing queers with little or no self-respect, twirling, bumping, shopping—whatever they call their new drug trips. Vocabularies are now full of letters—E, G, K, X— ad infinitum. The most popular gateway drug is no longer pot or coke but Serostim or creatine, or a host of other steroids used to make our bodies the epitome of perfect. Countless hours are devoted to the gym so we can have that perfect physique and then use that muscular bicep to pour alcohol into our system, chemicals into our bloodstream, and smoke into our lungs. If our internal organs were on the outside, perhaps we'd be more likely to take care of them too.

And we glorify the body, the lifestyle. Magazines are devoted to it. Parties are planned all over the country around it. Look through any chat room, online classified ad, or publication and all you'll see is "Gym buddy seeks same" Or the even better notion, "straight-acting." Who wants to spend their lives acting? I'm gay—what's wrong with acting that way?

That's just a subculture, you say. That's not everyone. Really? Go to any Gay Pride event, *any,* and then disagree with me. Hundreds of thousands of shirtless men with perfect pecs—so generic, if you cut off their heads you'd never be able to identify their lifeless, chiseled bodies—being stepped over by campy drag queens or lesbians on Harleys wearing only nipple caps and leather vests.

And let's talk about sex, baby. I slept with an HIV-positive man for nearly 12 years. I, we, lived with the trials and tribulations of AIDS daily—the CTs, MRIs, gallium scans, lumbar punctures, five pills up to 25 pills a day, side effects, flying halfway across the country for drug studies, the uncertainty of "Is this just a cold or the beginning of the end?" Through it all we had wonderful, exciting sex, and yes, I'm still HIV-negative. Safer sex works. So it came as a shock to me that five minutes into a Gay.com Long Beach online chat room someone asked me to come over and bareback. It came as a bigger shock when one of my best friends admitted that in the last six months he's allowed not one but two men to actually finish the job inside of him without a condom. He deserved the 10 days of anguish waiting for his results (this time he got lucky).

When the Centers for Disease Control and Prevention announced recently that AIDS cases are rising and that the number one group of new infections is gay men ages 16–25, I thought, There has to be something in the Aquafina. Anyone over the age of 15 who contracts HIV deserves it. They are ignorant to a disease that has been around over 20 years. And if they are gay and male, they doubly deserve it. We've seen firsthand what it can do and choose to ignore that for our own carnal desires.

Bathhouses are still open. How ridiculous is that? And gay men still flock to them. Not you? Not anyone you know? You'd be surprised. Perhaps you're a member of the coffee-house clique—the liberated guy who likes to read, go to plays and movies, and have a nice dessert with friends. Ten minutes after sitting down at The Library here in Long Beach three conversations around me turned to sex, drugs, or the gym. A half hour at Coffee Haven and already a gentleman had offered me his company, for a price.

Perhaps we're not all sex-obsessed, gym-going, straight-acting, self-loathing beings. Perhaps the years of us being browbeaten and told we were inferior hasn't affected us. Maybe not having legal rights or benefits hasn't damaged our cultural psyche so much, and maybe we are "just like everyone else."

Yeah, and perhaps George W. Bush could explain the theory of relativity in detail.

So what? you say. So that's just a part of who we are and we should embrace it…what harm does it cause?

A lot. As I stood in the Californian state capitol in Sacramento, about to testify in front of the senate judiciary committee in support of AB 25—a bill that grants 13 legal benefits to domestic partners—I listened to the opposition's attack. And I had a big problem. I couldn't defend us against the attacks because what the right-wing Christian zealot was saying was, in fact, true. If the members of that panel had a preconceived notion of who and what gay people are, it's because we have bought into it. We feed it to them.

Attitude about or perception of a culture can cause harm in more ways than you could ever imagine. I will go to my grave believing the perception of the gay male community contributed to the death of Andrew. It was Long Beach Gay Pride weekend, 200,000 gays and lesbians in town—some of them doing drugs or too much alcohol and ending up in the emergency room. We showed up at 4 A.M. and my partner had a seizure right there. From that moment on the only question the ER staff cared about was "What drugs was he using?" Countless times we were asked. Of course he had to be using drugs. He was young, healthy, buff, obviously gay…so the first conclusion was *Here's another drugged-out queer.*

He wasn't drugged out. He was having a heart attack.

They never even looked. But that night, that weekend, so many gay men *were* drugged out. This had to be one more.

We can't pull together as a community because we have no sense of it. We have no real leaders. We hear from GLAAD all the time, protecting our interests in the entertainment industry. So what do we get on national TV? A show about drugged-out bar boys or a straight-acting gay man with a female best friend and a raging queen as his neighbor. Good work, GLAAD, I feel comforted knowing you're looking out for us. That same group has never once mentioned my name, and yet I still sit as one of the only openly gay talk-show hosts in the country, on the number one radio station in the number two market in the nation, with an audience of more than five million nongay listeners.

And as for the Human Rights Campaign, gay centers, and such, how much do they play a role in most of our lives? Most of us don't frequent them, don't stay in touch with what they're doing, and have only a passing interest.

It's a shame gay men have come to this as a culture. We have such hope, such brilliance. But why would society grant us anything? Because it's the right thing to do? Since when does society do what's moral as a whole? We need to prove we deserve it. And all we do is fall back to the methods of being gay from an archaic past when sex was dirty and clandestine, when it was acceptable to be an underground culture. I don't see many single gay men doing much of all that these days.

Yes, these are generalizations. In general, we are promiscuous. In general, we abuse more substances. In general, we are narcissistic. And in general, that is how we are perceived. Trust me. I talk to thousands of nongays a week, meet them, get e-mails from them. Their first line is invariably "I had no idea that there were gay people like you out there": gay men who disagree with the path their own culture is taking. It's a shame I now have more in common with my nongay friends than my gay ones.

Perhaps a new class is emerging: HomoHetero. Single gay men someplace in the middle. Gay men who don't agree with the way things are going. Gay men who realize sex is good, a nice evening of partying is fine, but all in moderation. And gay men who realize we've become exactly what they said we were, and now it's going to take a lot longer to get the equality that as humans we deserve but that as a culture we seem destined to never achieve, due to our own actions.

Two Has to Be
Better Than One

The year 2001 was less than stellar. Going into it I was all set: I loved the movie *2001* so I figured any day now we'd have videophones and hovercrafts. Instead we had the greatest act of terrorism ever perpetrated against the United States. We had recession. We had the repercussions of the election process. Personally, I lost my partner of nearly 12 years. Hell, even my 16-year-old cat died in February.

Not a good year at all.

So we enter 2002 a nation at war with terror. We also enter it a gay community still at war with lawmakers and right-wing political groups, a community seeing a second epidemic of our old friend AIDS, and one composed of more narcissists than any other sect. And yet there's hope, and joy, and a promise of a better year ahead.

The year 2001 saw the passing of the most important piece of legislature in the country since Vermont's civil unions law, California's AB 25. It also saw a growing acceptance of gay and lesbian–favorable programs and characters on national television as well as recognition for the gay heroes of the September 11 tragedy. We saw great unification both in and out of the gay community and renewed our sense in the human spirit.

So what about 2002? As we all sit and plan, think, make resolutions, I thought it would be interesting to share mine. One thing 2001 taught us is that we are all far more alike than we are different. So perhaps some of these resolutions will inspire you, make you laugh, or confirm that I'm a total idiot.

#1: The Whole Weight Thing. The number one resolution in the United States is to lose weight. I've made it countless times and finally, two years ago, did something about it. So I lost 80 pounds through a program called Lindora and by learning to work out again. I felt great, and people said I looked great. Then Andrew died and the gym got dusty and the chocolate began to flow and 20 pounds found me. And now, seven months later, I realize all I've ever done is make excuses for my weight, and I'm using grief as another. I'm fat because I want to be and so are you. We all know what works (eat right, exercise) and then use excuses to not get to it. "Oh, I've got to write this column today, I don't have time..." "Oh, I've worked too hard today to get in that gym..." "Oh, I'll be bad this weekend and then get back to basics on Monday..."

We all give a lot of people a lot of our time each day. And then we put us last. Well, this year, it's back to me, so to speak. I've restarted my Lindora program and I've started working out. I resolve I will continue doing this, and I resolve to lie to myself and say it's for me when it's really because there's some personal appearance coming up that I must look great for, or some guy whom I may want to impress with a svelte me.

#2: Personal Presumptions. In my business, everyone presumes they know who you are and what you're going to say. We all make presumptions about people quickly, within seconds of meeting them. We may base this on looks, personality, clothing, or friends. I'm the worst at this. You see, I loathe circuit boys. Well, I thought I did. I presumed they were all drugged-out messes with no lives except the gym and the dance floor, with a quick trip to Mexico for some K or E. Then one night I had the most interesting political conversation with a gorgeous, buff boy named Doug. Found out he's considering finishing his master's degree in psychology. Two days later I'm debating the role and responsibilities gay politicians have to their community with Ken C., a guy who could have just modeled for *Muscle and Fitness* and who is finishing his Ph.D. work.

What? A brain? Well, that blows my whole presumption. What's more, the fact that they chose to talk to me blows my theory that guys like them don't even look at guys like me. To top it all off, I found myself reflecting on the conversations and wishing to talk with these guys again. Then my friend David marries a guy he met at one of these circuit parties. What do you know—he's the kindest, gentlest man I think I've met in some time. And he treats my friend well.

We all have ways of getting by in this life. Facades are a major factor in getting by. Some of us choose to be loud, flamboyant, blond, and bold in an attempt to be who we feel we are, while others devote time to their bodies and their outward appearance. But there are some things that don't get developed by pumping iron: mind and personality, kindness and love, vulnerability and strength. These all are housed in and worked on inside the soul. People with ripped stomachs and bulging biceps have a soul too, it would appear. At least some of them. So I resolve: no more presumptions about people that are based solely on my preconceived notions. You could miss some fabulous people that way.

And part B of this resolution is that I will no longer be surprised when one of these people actually pays attention to me. Why wouldn't they? It appears that we all have the same guidelines: Window dressing is nice, but the whole person is more interesting. I resolve to also continually tell myself that it's the real person that counts, what's inside, when the male stripper is waving his thong three inches from my face on the dance floor of the Fire Island bar.

And as a final resolution: I resolve to give myself a break sometimes. We all beat ourselves up so much, we don't really need others to do it for us. In today's society we don't cut many people much slack, least of all ourselves. So I will resolve to give myself a little more leeway. I'm human—so are you, if you're reading this—and human, by nature, means imperfect. So I resolve to give myself the same breaks I'd give someone I love. We can, sometimes, only do what we can. So cut a break to yourself every so often. And then cut your lover or friend one. Hell, even once, cut your boss one. You'll see stress just leave the building. And I resolve that when I cut myself these breaks, I will only obsess over only five things instead of 10.

2001 brought enough stress for a decade.

2002 could bring enough change for a lifetime.

You Can't Say
That Either!

If you're gay or lesbian, you'd better watch your mouth. After all, freedom of speech may apply to you in theory—as do the many other rights under the Constitution that allegedly apply to you but truly never seem to—yet in practice, you need a network censor. That is, if you don't want to step on any toes, cross any lines, or heaven forbid, play into a stereotype. In fact, if you are gay or lesbian, there's a host of topics you must never discuss because your opinion doesn't count—the masses will tune you out simply because of your sexuality.

This concept is not new to me, but I was reminded of it recently by one of my producers, Matt Seyden. You see, singer R. Kelly had just been indicted on 21 counts of child pornography for having sex with a 16-year-old on video (the idiot—never film such things in America when you're a celebrity!). That day I was making my second appearance on CNN's *Talkback Live*! I was researching the subject in case host Arthel Neville brought up the topic. I wanted to talk about the age-of-consent laws in this country and how ludicrous I believe them to be. Matt's warning lights went off, and he immediately said, "Oh, no, not another fag talking about how it should be legal to have sex with children. They'll tune you right out."

I was outraged. But it wasn't the first time I had heard this. At KFI, I was often told to pick my topics carefully. Don't have a strong opinion on religion, because the audience expects you to be an atheist. Don't criticize the Republicans too much, because people expect a gay person to be liberal and will just not listen. Don't tackle the gay marriage bill, because everyone knows you're for it.

I suppose when I started sucking dick I stopped having valid opinions on many, many topics. It's obvious that all gays and lesbians share the same opinions on so many topics that we shouldn't even discuss them, because everyone just *knows* what we're going to say and that makes it less credible. Give me a break.

The age-of-consent laws are a joke. In the United States alone there are over seven different age-of-consent laws, from 14 in Iowa to 18 in California (according to www.ageofcon-sent.com). I guess kids in Iowa mature more quickly than those in California. Thank God for second cousins. But Matt didn't want me to say this because he thought no one would hear it from me. All they would think is that I, an almost 40-year-old gay man, wants sex with a minor. Please, I look the other way passing the local high school. I like men full grown, thank you.

When I wanted to have an author on my show whose book suggests that the U.S. adopt the same policy as the Netherlands in terms of age of consent, my producer told me it was a bad idea. In the Netherlands age of consent is 12 to 16 as long as it is consensual and no one disapproves; after 16, completely legal. Studies suggest this does not adversely affect the child, nor does it lead to more pregnancies or molestations. And as a result the Dutch don't pay to put away people whose only offense is looking at nude pictures of a 16-year-old. But wait, that sounds like an opinion, and as a gay man I'm not supposed to have one on this subject.

Each and every day we are reminded of how limited we are as U.S. citizens when it comes to equality under the law. Each and every day we are reminded that socially it is still safer to stay among ourselves and thus live, and sometimes work, in very pro-gay environments surrounded by others like us. And each and every day it would appear we have to censor our speech because our point of view is not only expected but invalid.

I say, so what? So what if some of our views are expected? Yes, I am agnostic. I don't buy into religion. Not because I'm gay but because I don't like fairy tales and I don't have to prove a negative. I am more analytical, scientific. Afterlife? Perhaps, but not as painted by the multibillion-dollar corporations that call themselves churches. Religion is government, always has been. But making that statement as a gay man—well, I know, it doesn't count. As for politics, one of the reasons it was hard to book me on *Politically Incorrect* was because they never knew where I'd be on a topic. In the producer's own words, "You're Democrat on some, Republican on others, Libertarian on even more..." So much for the stereotype there.

I'm about common sense, not affiliations. Oops, another opinion.

So I guess this means we shouldn't take any fried chicken recipes from a black person, never talk to an Asian about driving safety, and tune out any Christian who happens to talk about a gay issue. After all, we know where they're coming from, so why bother? Their opinions don't count.

We are many things. We are diverse. So are our opinions. So are the things we like to talk about in public or private. Censoring ourselves because it may be deemed predictable is just another way some would choose to remind us that we don't fit in. I say poppycock. Voice your opinion. If most tune out, so what? Someone will be listening. One person may get something out of it. And it's that person you want to connect with because that's the person who sees beyond sexuality and realizes individuals have opinions that aren't connected to their genitalia.

Anti-Gay Sentiments
Right on Target

Since when did the gay community, the most fashion-conscious group on the planet, start wearing large bull's-eye targets? It had to be sometime in the late '70s, since that is when it appears that all real forward movement stopped in the equality department. Now we've become a community of easy targets, one that has shots taken at it every day and just sits there and says, "Thank you, sir, may I have another?"

Now, before all you gay bleeding-heart activists come unglued, face it: For every step forward taken, five steps backward are forced upon us. Matthew Shepard is dead, and nothing has changed. Absolutely nothing. We thought he was the battle cry for the '90s, the personification of the movement for the new millennium. But alas, he was just an unfortunate soul who was killed, a media sound bite and a rally point for antiquated groups of activists. Hate crimes are on the rise in most urban areas, not decreasing; hate-crimes laws on a federal level aren't gaining support; and according to a survey by Who's Who of American High Schools, bigotry in young people has risen 19%. Equal marriage rights have been defeated in many states and stand to take a beating in others in years to come. Religious zealots can still call us evil and wrong on national television with no repercussions whatsoever, and our sexuality is continually being put up to a public vote in some fashion for approval or disapproval. Imagine, sexuality by consensus.

Negativity is everywhere. Log on to the Internet at any given moment. Go to one of 15 Web sites that deal exclusively with gay and lesbian news. Two thirds of what is presented is bad news about laws being defeated that would help us, new laws being made to restrict us, or various attacks against us. Why? Because we're easy targets. Like shooting fish in a barrel. And please don't counter me with a plethora of "But look how far we've come, we've now got" blah blah blah blah blah. Get a clue.

And don't be so quick to point the "they're out to get us" finger at the mainstream. We have become our own worst enemies. We are so disempowered as a community it is almost ludicrous to call ourselves one. Unity in the gay community is a myth. There is no national consensus as to what is best for us, no great leader to rally our support. Where is our Martin Luther King Jr., our Jesse Jackson, our Gandhi? Even our leading organizations like the Human Rights Campaign and National Gay and Lesbian Task Force spend more time on internal politics and flashpoint issues than they do actually making a difference in the day-to-day life here at this homestead. And our media has replaced images of Shepard with George Michael. Better sales.

On a smaller level, one would think that post-Shepard there would be a cry for safety in the gay male community: a call for morality, ethics, and common sense where something as simple as choosing a sex partner is concerned. But no, things still go on the same. Every night thousands of gay men are going home with total strangers, hopping into the car, truck, or sports-utility vehicles of some unknown figure just because his package looks good in jeans or he said something nice. And why bother even hopping into a car? Why not just go out back, run off to the bathroom, or cavort in a dark alley that would make Superman think twice before entering it? Parks are still full of horny queers on the dick trail, people willing to follow others into the bushes or clandestine buildings to get off. One mile from my house is a beach known as a cruising spot. Drive through there at any time of day and you can find someone willing to either eat there or takeout. Not even a name is required.

"That's not me," you're exclaiming. "That's a small segment of our group, the ones who give us a bad name."

Grow up. Go to West Hollywood, New York, South Beach, wherever more than 10 gay men meet, and you'll find risky behavior. Men going home with strangers, looking for Mr. Goodbar. Of course we're victims—we set ourselves up to be time and again.

And please don't dish me any of the reasoning that we behave this way because we have low self-esteem due to years of browbeating from the mainstream community. Stop it, that's too easy. It gets us out of our responsibility. We don't need another note from Mother to excuse our behavior. We need to drink a large bottle of Act Right and realize that we have been so busy fighting for others to not inflict their morality on us that we forgot to develop one of our own.

This applies to many areas, not just sex. As we fight for the right to marry, our relationships can be different, special, with certain concessions or "arrangements." One member of a "married" couple sat on my sofa not four days ago and happily told us how his husband had just called him from Houston on the way to a bathhouse with two men he had just met. Meanwhile, the partner here was off to a beer bust. Call me old-fashioned, but that was one of the saddest things I had ever heard. No wonder we can't win the right to marry; we can't even define it. Isolated? Pla-a-a-e-e-ez. And let's not talk about the safety issues of the wayward partner going off with two men in a rental car to a bathhouse. Bet there were a few cocktails involved.

One of our pop stars gets arrested for public sex and he gets more press than his failing career deserves. Granted, I love his candor, his honesty, and some of his music. But has any one public person condemned the action? Suddenly he's the patron saint of Project Angel Food.

Our porn stars go legit and do nude theater and call it "real." The pretense of art is used as an ethical thong for what is simply soft-core porn. Great theatrical representation there, guys. Not to mention the thousands of pages of copy these endeavors get, surpassing any manifesto or agenda. And gay men flock to the theaters around the country to support these shows. We really are just our sexuality, aren't we? If not, we look like it.

How on earth can we expect the public's perception of us to change from that of immoral sodomites to productive members of society if we can't even change that image within our own community? We risk our lives for sex; if a societal rule is constricting to us, we ignore it. We present blatant sexual imagery as legitimate art and media—and what's worse, when someone beats on us, we moan a little and move on.

I am not one of the fortunate who can live among the gay cultural elite, where everyone is an activist, a new battle won each week, and everyone is so optimistic about our future. You see, I am forced to live in the real world. I'm not in a gay ghetto; I'm in an urban center open to everyone. In the past year I've had things thrown at my car because of my rainbow triangle, fielded thousands of disapproving calls on my radio show, and feared for my safety while simply eating dinner next to some radical youths. So while thousands march on Washington to be greeted by an empty White House, I live in a world where Pat Robertson and years of hatred still make the rules. How can I expect anything else when my own community isn't fighting for its life with every means available? The threat is not being met with an equal force of resistance.

Jews and African-Americans caught on a long time ago, and look where they are in their movements. Anti-Semitic remarks are no longer acceptable in our media or television because they have litigated their way to equality. The word *nigger* has now become the *n* word for the same fear of political correctness and fear of repercussion. Ah, yes, fear. Who's afraid of the gay community? No one. Not a soul. We carry the political and social clout of perhaps the American Indian. And at least they get casinos.

Granted, the gay community has become a market, but fiscally forceful? Not! Our boycotts seldom work (except where alcohol is concerned, since we drink so damned much of it per capita). Not to mention that as a community we never stick to them. How many of you shop at JCPenney, eat at Wendy's or Carl's Jr., drink Coors? You get the picture. And as for the religious right, why should they care if they spew hatred? Who has the money to fight them?

Well, they can be named as litigants. They can be fought. The burden of proof is on them to supply substantial evidence that the Bible is not a work of fiction and that their hatred is not simply another fund-raising gimmick.

If you've read this far, you either agree or want me dead. How dare I say that we are victims? We are targets! How dare I call us immoral? Sorry to those out there who are wonderful, well-rounded, moral individuals. Problem is, your voice is so seldom heard. Perhaps you could pop out of the fund-raisers or politically correct board meetings long enough to be heard.

As for the post-gay movement, I agree in theory, but once again conclude that we haven't learned how to be a unified gay community yet, so how can we move beyond it? As I hear *postgay,* the only post I think of is the one Matthew was tied to. We can't move beyond what we haven't mastered.

Where is it going? Downhill, fast, if we don't mobilize in a big way. I mean *big,* on a broad scale, litigate the hell out of every religious fantastic who would cause us pain. Become a social and economic force through stronger unity, which means that our leaders need to remove their heads from their posteriors and find a way to reach the mainstream gay community. On a smaller scale, how about growing up? Let's stop being the bratty stepchild—willful, ignorant of the real world.

Let's remove the targets from our backs and begin taking aim ourselves. How? There's a million people to tell you that. But you'd better do something quick. I'm getting tired of taking all the crap as an openly gay person. I grow weary of the hatred that seems so prevalent at times. And I'm getting a little sick of the preponderance of gay men out there who think life is one big circuit party or that commitment can be redefined on a daily basis. I am not asking for religious morality, simply common sense. Remember that? Don't get into cars with strangers. Don't do the same thing over and over again and expect different results. Consensus before action. Don't look to expand until things are right at home.

Common sense for an uncommon community.

Summer Parties or Season of Pride?

Brush off your nipple rings, stitch up your sequins, and power down some steroids, it's that time of year again. That's right, the season of Pride is upon us, as all around the country the dykes are mounting their bikes, the bars are decking out their flatbed trucks, and the church groups are lining up behind the AIDS organizations that are nestled between the hard bodies and recovery groups—all parading down Main Street USA.

It is a time of year when we come together as a community, to celebrate the events that took place so many years ago at a little bar in New York City, the Stonewall Inn, when a group of drag queens said "enough is enough" and stood up for their rights. That simple act of rebellion inspired a splintered community to come together at least once a year to show the rest of the world that we are one, we are strong, we are proud.

Well, at least in theory. What's really happened is that we've created events that are part circuit party, part dragfest, part sexual fetishes on parade, and part just plain embarrassing.

Perhaps it's because Pride became so successful. Perhaps it's because we lost sight of the goal. Whatever the reason, there's not much to be proud about anymore at our Pride events. Having attended hundreds across the country as both a spectator and participant, it has now become my distinct pleasure to avoid the events at all costs. I've grown weary of trying to explain them to my nongay friends, tired of us feeding the freakish news bites that invariably run at 11 P.M.— you know, the Sisters of Perpetual Indulgence followed by lesbians with their nipple rings to the wind and one too many heterosexual has-been disco stars for my taste.

It's not that I haven't tried to enjoy them. My late partner Andrew and I were asked to emcee to emcee the Los Angeles Christopher Street West Pride Parade for television. Halfway through the event we took an almost comedic tone, because we just couldn't rationalize 20 half-naked men on a flatbed truck, beer logos abounding, gyrating away to this or that disco song, representing this or that bar, followed by an AIDS service group and then a church. Every time a seven-foot drag queen walked by with nothing but a T-string on, we couldn't help but comment how proud we were to be gay men at that moment.

There were no floats, no real ones, yet this was the second-largest parade in California. Aren't we supposed to be creative? There were no contingencies of doctors, lawyers, playwrights, authors, major workers' unions...nothing, just a lot of the same. It was fetishes on parade and the occasional straight group like PFLAG to rally the crowd.

Of course, when we mentioned this, we were shunned. When we asked why we praise parents and friends of gays for doing exactly what any normal person, whether parent, friend, or otherwise, should do—accept and love their gay or lesbian child, sibling, or friend, we were tuned out. When we questioned why the headliner at Las Vegas Pride, Cyndi Lauper, got a sizable fee, limo service, and a hotel suite while the gay and lesbian acts got to get dressed alongside a Porta

Potti, drive themselves, and sleep where they may, we were told it was none of our business. And when we posed the question that perhaps the grand marshal should at least be a gay man or lesbian instead of some accepting heterosexual, we were told we didn't know what we were saying.

In fact, the Christopher Street West organization threatened our radio station, KFI, with a lawsuit if we didn't retract some of our statements about the Pride festivities. Us, the only openly gay people on the radio, the gay guys whose show aired after Dr. Laura and Rush Limbaugh—we got the threat of a lawsuit. The right-wing Christian groups left us alone, as did the anti-gay Republicans and the legions of non-gay people who would want us off the air. They never once drafted proposals against us. It was the gay group that gave us grief. Because we spoke out with a contrary opinion.

The truth is, Gay Pride events have become a joke. They should remove the word *pride* from their titles and just be called what they are, Big Gay Parties. The community itself is becoming splintered, with more and more gays and lesbians opting out of the festivities.

Gay Pride weekend in Long Beach is in May. That weekend in 2001 is when I lost my partner. So this year, 2002, I didn't feel much like participating. So while the parade kicked off downtown, I went to Home Depot that Sunday to get some things for the backyard, my late husband's pride and joy. There I met Tim, an old friend, who was shopping for lattice with his husband. A few minutes later John and Steve were found in the lighting department, getting a new dining room fixture. The parade was going full steam not five miles away, and here they were, shopping at Home Depot. And I realized: That was their Pride event. Making a home for themselves, their family. Being together, a visible couple, integrated into the community. And that touched a nerve.

Andrew and I used to have a rainbow triangle on our car. We never thought much about it. Then one day we had to go to a biker bar in Trabuco Canyon, Calif. A very famous and very rowdy place. On the way there several bikers passed, and more than a few expressed upset about our rainbow. When we got there we took it off. Now you're probably gasping. But you know what? We didn't need it anymore. You see, each day we went before millions of nongays, the happy gay couple talking about life, love, and current events. We were proud by example, by living as two out gay men in front of millions who then gained a better understanding of who and what gay people are. We didn't need the flag, the parade, a banner; we just needed to live openly.

We scream we are the same as our heterosexual counterparts, and then throw events to show them exactly how different we are. We put our sexual fetishes on parade in front of hundreds of thousands and call it Pride. We drink ourselves silly in beer tents, dance with half-naked muscle-bound boys at parties sponsored by AIDS organizations while doing designer drugs—and feel we are expressing who we truly are. We support the heterosexual arts community by paying performers like Cyndi Lauper, Pat Benatar, and Crystal Waters, while gay and lesbian acts have to scrounge up money for airfare or hotel—yet we feel we have presented something balanced and well-rounded.

Gay Pride events are now business ventures—nothing more, nothing less. They don't become more because we don't demand more. Those who have outgrown them or lost interest simply don't attend, and those who love the party atmosphere, the countless trinket booths, beer vendors, and overpriced food stands plop down their money willingly. It's all economics, really.

Even I enjoy the electric atmosphere in the city when a Pride event is in town. The local clubs are full, more gays and lesbians are visible in the community as a whole, and there is a certain energy only strength in numbers can bring.

But there can be no doubt Pride events are now dinosaurs,

relics of a time gone by when our sexuality was so suppressed that we thought the only way to be proud was to wear it down the street in defiance. What's sad is that some of those attending aren't out at work or home; haven't learned how to have a committed relationship; don't realize that there is a great gay heritage of scientists, doctors, lawyers, politicians, adventurers, authors, CEOs, inventors, and countless others on which to draw. They don't see that Pride comes through everyday deeds, not a parade. That living out by example—that integrating, not segregating—is the ultimate act of pride. And that until we achieve equality under the law, we will be held to a higher standard, an unfair light and scrutiny; and that as long as we keep giving our detractors so much ammunition, we won't ever achieve those goals. Elevating what's best about our community isn't hard, it just isn't as glamorous. Promoting every aspect of who we are isn't impossible, it just doesn't play well in beer or dance tents. And presenting a more balanced picture to those from outside the community who would watch isn't a huge chore, but might require a major paradigm shift in thinking that we just don't seem willing to make.

Yet, hope springs eternal. June 2002 saw a new Pride event, one born in a country of war, of terror, of unrest: 250-plus people marched through Israel in that nation's first-ever Pride parade. They risked attack, retaliation; they had the military march alongside with automatic weapons. But they marched—they made their statement. The drag queens from Stonewall would be proud. Meanwhile, in California's conservative Orange County, this year its Pride event has been cancelled. A gay community of over 30,000 and it can't support one event. All the better: Their parade never even touched city property; it was held at a college in the middle of nowhere. You win some, you lose some.

Be who you are. And be proud. Just be sure to present the whole picture instead of a snapshot of who we are in the bed room or barroom.

My Big Gay Moments

I am quite sure that there have been many historically significant moments throughout gay history—the start of the Stonewall riots, Ellen's coming-out, the invention of water-soluble lubricant—that helped shape or define us as a movement. However, it's the little moments, the unreported incidents that shape and define us as people and end up being the best reminders that being gay is in fact still one of the most enjoyable things on the planet.

For instance, just yesterday I was in the kitchen baking a cake for a Fourth of July party. It was "red velvet" cake, an intricate recipe that produces a blood-red cake, white icing, and blueberry trim. How patriotic. I had on my chef's coat (I found it and a hat at Pic 'N' Save for under $20 once) and apron and had the full arsenal of tools out, including the monster KitchenAid mixer. It was time to frost. So, there were were, my best friend Karen and me, frosting and applying blueberries. Popera diva Emma Shapplin's debut release *Carmine Meo* was playing over the stereo directly out of iTunes (I've digitized all my CDs and then filed them away)— a modern-day opera sung by a 24-year-old French girl and produced by an American trance-ambient producer. At that moment I stopped, looked at Karen, and stated, "I'm listening to popera, frosting my red velvet cake, which is color-coordinated for the Fourth of July, in a chef's coat surrounded by every kitchen convenience in the world. I'm so gay."

Yes, it was a big gay moment. There have been others. My late husband Andrew and I had them all the time.

I collect boxes. Andrew bought me the ultimate box, a large hand-carved mammoth-bone chest. He decided it needed to stay open. So one morning he woke up, got me motivated, and out the door we had to dart. The phone rang. It was our friend Emily. Andrew immediately got on the phone and said, "We don't have time to talk right now. We have to go out in search of lots of pretty pillows for our chest, and perhaps a chenille throw. Cost Plus always has pretty pillows and throws. But we have to hurry to get the best selection." I looked at him and assured him no heterosexual male had made that statement in the last 10 years. Definitely a big gay moment.

They happen to everyone eventually. While at the dinner party for which the cake was intended, my two dear friends Ken and Dennis relayed the most recent drama of their beachfront high-rise. It appears a soldering iron caught fire in the unit upstairs and the unit was blazing—fire erupting in a high-rise. The alarms were sounding. The fire department was shouting over bullhorns to evacuate, that this was not a drill. Ken gathered a few things in the bedroom. Dennis grabbed some papers. They headed for the door. Then Dennis looked at Ken and said, "Wait a minute. You're not wearing a gray shirt too? Hold on." He put down his treasures as the fire raged, darted into the bedroom, and changed shirts. Yes, another case of a very big gay moment.

If you're gay, you have these moments too. And it's time we pay a little more attention to them. You see, being gay is a blast. Contrary to public belief, we are not all depressed, oppressed, self-absorbed, substance-abusing narcissists. We don't all live under the gray cloud of the AIDS epidemic, the upset that can come from the tyranny of an American political system that refuses to accept us as equals, the drama that infidelity can bring. Oh, sure, those things are around. And at times it appears they are the gay community. But they're not. We have to separate the very essence of being gay from the politics and perception of it.

Because when it all boils down to it, those fabulously fun gay moments, not the sex that we have, are what make us who we are. I have always maintained that a person can be celibate and still be gay, or have never engaged in gay sex and identify as gay. And recently someone has been spreading the rumor that being gay is a drag; whoever is spreading that rumor is straight.

Identify your big gay moments. Revel in them, and cherish them. Realize that they are a big part of who you are. Live each day knowing that this life isn't a burden but a gift. I mean, really, we do have more fun than our nongay counterparts. Think of all the interesting and exotic situations we leave ourselves open to throughout life—situations that straight men or women could never even conceive of, let alone see the humor or fun in them. And laugh at yourself. When I did my radio show on KFI with Andrew, he would stop me dead in the middle of a sentence on major-market radio and say, "You are so gay..." Oh, sure, I might have been raving about a new singer or ranting about the impossibility of finding affordable 320-thread-count sheets, but it didn't matter. Right then and there he stopped me for a moment and pointed out what a big homo I am. And it wasn't a bad thing; it was a fun thing.

Have a sense of humor about yourself and your big gay moments. Laugh out loud when you catch them; share them with others. Be proud of them all year long. As a community we've forgotten how to laugh. We've almost hidden our big gay moments in an effort to blend. I say incorporate them. Laugh with your straight friends at your differences, hell; make them jealous that they're not part of such a fun club. Because I don't know about you, but even now, as I approach 40, I still find that being gay is a blast, and truth be told, I wouldn't have it any other way.

Island of Misfit Toys

It happens every year in homes all across America. As millions sit down to watch parades and football and prepare to feast on roast beast while surrounded by loved ones, others laugh and dance in the kitchen while reciting lines from *All About Eve*. *Holidays* are a time for gatherings and family. To most of America that means in-laws they never see, relatives they wish they didn't have to see, and the perennial argument, "But we went to your mother's house last year—this year we have to go to..."

It is also time for unconventional gatherings, the Islands of Misfit Toys, the gays and lesbians who throw down a spread for their "extended" family—a unit of people drawn together not out of blood but out of love and the need to "be" someplace on Thanksgiving or Christmas.

Now, as the elder statesmen of gay couples, my partner Andrew and I were that island. Each and every year for the past 11 years Andrew would create a sumptuous feast and the open invitation went out to our friends. Each year dinner for 10 or more was served. Many showed up early in the day; others came just for pie or dessert as a way to escape the traditional family hell they'd been in the rest of the day.

The gatherings became a regular event, and it gave those people who attended a sense of belonging, a place to be. In fact, when one of our dear friends moved to Hawaii, we videotaped our gatherings all day long—just let the camera run—and sent the hours of tape to her so she could still spend the day.

There were those whose family lived far away and they couldn't afford to travel that year. There were others who had no wish to be with their real family on Thanksgiving or Christmas because their partners weren't welcomed or they would have to hide their relationship. Some came because we *were* their family, not by blood but by the unbreakable bond of friendships forged through years of good and bad times.

It gave Andrew and I such a great sense of family and love. Preparation was often hectic: changing the menu each year (hint...never try eggplant with Gruyère cheese sauce), getting the right party favors, music, games, videos, adding to the guest list right up until dinner. The mix was always vibrant— from my senior mother to our circuit boy friends; from those who had to rush off to do drag shows to those who were betting on the various games. It was a group one might never find together anyplace else but at the dinner table on Thanksgiving or on the patio on Christmas afternoon.

Something miraculous happened over those years of hosting holiday misfits. Soon there were no misfits—there was a family. New members were brought in, as some changed lovers or gained new ones; some seats were left empty for those that had been lost during the previous year. And the day seemed normal. Yes, normal. Just like a regular Christmas or Thanksgiving. Andrew would be madly cooking; I would be assisting along with other friends in the kitchen. A group would be outside listening to music, having cocktails, lighting joints, whatever moved them to holiday cheer. Some were glued to the TV, arguing over whether to watch the *I Love Lucy* or *Twilight Zone* marathons. Fights erupted and were quelled, and by the end of the day everyone sat full, happy, and having that glow that only spending the day with family can give.

Now this year I am the misfit toy. Andrew is gone. Everyone expects the island to sink. But the beauty of it is, it can't. You see, the bonds we, and you, forge on those days don't go away. The extended family that gathers in the homes of those who have been made to feel outside the realm of normal family the rest of the year stays in place, even when one of the matriarchs fall. Because that's what we became. You all have a couple in your lives as well. The two lesbians who always invite you over. The two gay men who insist on hosting holiday events, like the annual Christmas party at their house or the usual Thanksgiving potluck. This year I host the event, with a little more help from friends and the same amount of love around the room.

To those who question our family values as a community, I say to them, Attend just one of these gatherings this year. You see, they are more precious than any "real" family gathering. Love is what brings us together the need to belong. The need to share. It's not blood, not obligation, not some warped sense of yearly duty that makes us sit at a table with those we would not normally see.

To those who have shared our gatherings over the years, my heartfelt thanks. To those who will join in future, welcome. And to those of you who find yourself host to the misfit toys of the world, know that you are doing something that forever touches and changes the lives of those who attend, even in such a small way.

Holidays are for families. I am so proud to be a member of a community that acknowledges that by creating families from the most unlikely of people in the most unusual of ways. Happy Holidays, be you misfit or matriarch. And Andrew, we'll still be setting a place for you here.

Being Human

We're human. There, it's been said. We are all human. Look in the mirror, grab yourself (no, it's not that kind of party) and admit it: You're human. Silly to mention, you say? Not so, if you look around in today's world. So much of our society is built around trying to limit, erase, or confine our humanity.

Why? Because being human means we have emotions. In fact, it means our lives are dictated by emotions. We have frailties, we are vulnerable, and we don't like it. That's why we have courts telling mothers they can't smoke around their children. We deem it a mistake, and we want to make sure no one makes mistakes, so we have a judge making high-handed decisions. We legislate what is decent and moral to protect ourselves from ourselves. We sit and scratch our heads over the Middle East, knowing all the while the conflict will never end because humans are involved and humans hate for no reason other than hatred for hatred's sake.

We try to compartmentalize our humanity, put it away. But it never works. How often have you gone to work with your mind on your other half? How much of your day is spent worrying about this or that argument? *Why hasn't that person called or e-mailed? Who am I going to see this weekend? Does my boss really like me?* Emotions, all of it.

The most important thing to any human is love. It's hard to believe that many would consider that a controversial statement. Some disagree. But truth be told, we spend our lives either looking for it, denying it, or reveling in it. As humans it's one of the things we cannot live without. It's like air, water, food. It feeds us, replenishes us, drives us crazy. It has inspired more works of art, more literature, more fights, more killings, and more joy than any other human emotion.

But in our society we have stripped love of its core and made it something else, and it hasn't served us well. Many look at love as work—it's not; it's play. It is not something that causes constant pain or requires constant attention. It is something that should be as effortless as breathing and as rewarding as life itself. We have convinced ourselves that we can live without it; we can be strong individuals who don't need anyone else to complete us. What a fallacy. What an empty shell of a human. Humans are social animals. We are meant to couple. It's who we are, no matter how we run from it.

We trivialize our humanity, denying it all the time. We don't make time for friends, for family, for lovers, husbands and wives. We let our work pull us away when we should be home. We let our careers be our spouses. We deny ourselves joy because of some warped concept that life isn't supposed to be simple, that it is all so complex, that emotions are complex. They're not.

Being human isn't easy. Because to admit such means that we admit we are prone to conflict. That, as humans, we segregate. We do. Like sticks with like. Everyone is inherently prejudiced; it's part of being human. Being human means we're not perfect, and no matter how we try and put this forced ideal in the forefront, we will never be perfect. All the laws in the world can be written to try and make us perfect, to try and make sure we always make the right decision, but we won't. We can't. It's not in our nature.

The concept of the perfect human has been brought to the forefront again thanks to, of all things, the Catholic Church. It has been embroiled in scandal, and why? Because people have found out that priests are human—and that an extremely small fraction of them make terrible mistakes. And then other humans involved did what anyone would do: try and protect their own, their organization, their very belief system. We're shocked that a cardinal would lie, because we don't want to admit that we ourselves would be capable of such lies given different circumstances. We condemn these things loudly, hoping the shouting will drown out the fact that we ourselves could be capable of equally terrible things. Because we're human.

But being human also means that we can grow, we can elevate to the next level—and that's the part we seem to have forgotten. Being human means we have the largest capacity of love and understanding of any creature on the planet. It means that in spite of it all, we can still find joy in the smallest of things—a flower, a smile, a sunset.

The problem with admitting we're all human is that we have to forgive ourselves and each other for it. We have to allow ourselves to be it. In this digital age, we want society and each other to function more like efficient machines than humans. Since that is impossible, we sometimes become a society of disappointment.

Being human is a finite thing; it doesn't last forever. Happy lives are afforded to those who realize their humanity early on, who embrace it, who see it as a great gift. The adage "But I'm only human" shouldn't be used to divert or excuse. What a miracle each and every one of us is, both biological and emotional. What marvelous things we are all capable of, and yes, what horrors. That all goes with being human. And what a binding force it can be. What a unifying factor, perhaps our only saving grace. We are all human, from Israeli to al-Qaeda, Catholic priest to gay boy next door. We do in fact have something in common with everyone. The sooner we all remember that, the sooner we can get on with the business of being human.

The Victims We Know So Well

The gay and lesbian community is filled with nothing but a bunch of powerless victims. Let me rephrase: If you are gay or lesbian in the United States, you are, in fact, a victim. At least that's the pabulum everyone from our political leaders to our media spew forth and we as a community buy up, buy into, and sell ourselves. We have sung in an oppressed chorus for so long that we have become victims of the very songs we sing.

Look around you—it's everywhere. Laws are constantly being passed to protect us—because, of course, we need special protection. Granted, legislation is needed to equal the playing field, but I don't believe that being gay falls under the Americans With Disability Act yet. Perhaps it should. Perhaps all offices should have to set aside a cubicle where it's safe to be gay, like for breast-feeding or a wheelchair-accessible bathroom. You know, we could decorate the cubicles, install mirror balls, water coolers (since most of us are on E and will need the hydration), plasma TV (to be able to watch the East Coast feed of *Queer as*

Folk), and mandatory 30-minute "dish" breaks every time some good gossip happens in the office.

Our gay and lesbian writers write us as victims. Just look at the masterminds behind the much touted second-season debut of *Queer as Folk, the only* show on television with more than two gay male characters that actually lets them *be* gay. Well, in a way. They actually let them be good victims.

Season opener: The out, proud happy gay youth gets bashed for having a grand time with a guy at his prom. Of course, all out, gay, happy, proud youths get bashed. Great message there. Then he gets brain damage, and the guy who does it gets a slap on the wrist, because we do in fact live in a society where you can hit any other human being in the head with a bat and get community service. Well, you can't hit any straight person, just gay youths, because we are in fact victims of hatred and bigotry, and there are no just judges or lawyers in the straight world who would find this appalling.

Of course, last season there was the happy couple, Michael and his doctor boyfriend. Well, they were happy until the writers of the only gay show on television brave enough to show a male-male relationship (will Will every *really* have a *positive, healthy* relationship on that other show?) decided that it was better to have them break up. Four gay men and two lesbians, and the *only* ones who get to have a positive, loving relationship for any length of time are the lesbians. Because gay men are incapable because we are victims of our own narcissism, emotional demands, and wandering penises.

We accept hate-crimes legislation being touted as progress because it hurts more when a bat strikes our skulls and the person says the word "faggot" or "kike" or "nigger." Protect us, for we are weak against those who would do us harm because of who we are. Guard us, for the evil justice system is set up to overlook or persecute us. Legislate for us, because we can't get jobs. Let us get married, because we're not valid without your seal of approval. *Give* us the rights we deserve, because we're not strong enough to *take* them. Protect us from AIDS, because we're too stupid to save ourselves from the disease. Care for us, because we are dying. Give us money, because we are sick. Love us, because we are different. Oh, but wait, we're the same.

This victim mentality has not served us well. We are not an empowered community; we are a community that still feels we are at the whim of public approval, the voting box, and sympathetic straight people. We can't get married because *they* keep voting against it…no, we can't get married because *we* are not voting *for* it. We don't mobilize, as we should. We get beaten because we don't make it unacceptable through legal retaliation; we don't demand, we wait for remedies. We forget the difference between someone who is a victim and someone who is oppressed. And there is a big difference.

I am *not* a victim, and to the politicians, authors, playwrights, guy next door, whomever, I say, Stop trying to make me feel that I am, because it's futile. I have a job I fought hard for, one they said I'd never keep, and I had a husband I cherished and a relationship that worked regardless of the laws that governed it. You can't oppress me if I refuse to be kept down. You may beat me out of hatred, but I will prosecute you out of justice and you *will* pay. If I believed we lived in a country where lawmakers and enforcement actually regularly allowed such things without repercussions, I'd move to Amsterdam. You may federally outlaw my unions, but I will fight that and win because of a document called the Constitution, one that *already* covers me, without any amendments to it regarding sexual orientation. Because I am an American. I'm already included.

The funny part is, so are all of you reading this. You've been sold the bill of goods for so long about being victims, you may believe it. It tears at our self-esteem (look at our drug and alcohol addiction rates, gay teen suicides, our lifestyle—is that a reflection of healthy self-esteem?). It keeps us unempowered because we believe we have to wait for someone to give us some power. We don't. We have it as Americans, we have it as humans, we have it for life.

So save your story lines where we never get the boy or we get beaten or oppressed. I'm over it. Those days are gone. This is 2002. Gay is no longer an issue for debate, it is a factual way of life. Rights are not to be deprived, they are to be taken. Love isn't only for them but for all of us as well. The victims we know so well may be ourselves, but we can turn that notion into being the survivors we can become once we all realize the only thing keeping us down is us.

So They Moved
Your Cheese

Hate it. Love it. Fear it. Avoid it. Prepare for it. Ignore it. Run from it. Accept it. Do what you will, it won't really matter, because change, my friends, is gonna come. Rely upon it happening. So it's not a matter of *if* things are going to change, just *when*. The real questions are "How are you going to deal with it?" and "Were you prepared for it?"

Change has surrounded me for 12 months. As I sit writing this I am less than two weeks away from the one-year anniversary of the loss of my partner, Andrew Howard. What a strange day May 21, 2001, was. I went from a one-word entity, CharlesandAndrew, to just Charles. The loss of love, of self, of stability—some of the greatest catalysts for change ever to exist. Then came the loss of my slot on KFI on April 12, 2002. Within 12 months of losing my husband my professional identity was lost as well. No longer would I be saying weekly, "I am Karel and this is KFI AM 640, more stimulating talk radio." Suddenly, my professional family was taken from me, right after the loss of my personal one. Now it's on to another station, KGO AM 810 San Francisco, television, the future. Great change.

So, in answer to question 1, how am I dealing with these changes? Well, some better than others. I thought a year ago I wouldn't cry as much as I still do about Andrew. People kept telling me it would get better, and I believed them. Well, it's a lie. Things don't get better. They change forever. There's a new state of "good." And while the shrink says that my progress is remarkable—making new friends, working, even thinking about an actual "date" (thinking, if nothing else)—I'm still not convinced. To any of you out there who have lost a partner, my hat's off to you. How you survived to read this is a miracle. Because it just hurts. And it's odd: As much as we realize things change, we have to realize that sometimes some things never will. Some pains will always hurt in any form.

Andrew's loss I couldn't see coming; no one can predict a mistake. But the loss of KFI I had to see coming, right? So why didn't I do something more about that? Because truth be told, I *didn't* really expect it. As much as I told myself that I saw it coming, it still caught me off-guard. I knew when a new program director arrived, I—or anyone doing a show— could be in danger. Everyone in radio knows that. And I didn't prepare. I hoped for the best. Sound familiar?

Maureen Smith, former head of Fox Family Channel, phoned me one day to talk about changing jobs in today's entertainment industry. She was in the middle of changing and knew I was as well. She told me about book called *Who Moved My Cheese?* by Spencer Johnson, MD. Everyone should read it. It's about dealing with change in your work and home life, and it hit home. Yes, I've been numb for the past 12 months, and that numbness is nowhere near wearing off. But I've also been dumb. I've been reactive instead of proactive. I've been waiting for things to change, knowing they will, and then dealing with the fallout instead of trying to guide the changes and protect myself when the course veers to a negative path.

So many times we see change coming—somebody "moves your cheese"—but ignore it. So many times we make bad decisions for ourselves either professionally or personally because it's easier than the alternative—great change. Often when great change happens, many of us go into paralysis of some kind—emotional, professional denial—and spend more time thinking about the unjustness of it all than dealing with the consequences of the change. We spend time thinking about how unfair it all is instead of trying to regain some control. We see the handwriting on the wall, but for some reason we think of it as art instead of words to heed. We see but don't comprehend.

Some people I know stay in dysfunctional relationships because neither can tip the boat over and make each other swim. Settling is easier than changing. Some I know stay at dead-end jobs, or jobs they hate, because of the fear of looking for a new one, the uncertainty of change, and the possibility of failure. Some see their job in jeopardy due to downsizing, conflicts at work, or mergers and yet don't prepare to move on before they're forced to do so. Others avoid conversations because they fear the outcome and the change it would bring. Some ignore negative behavior patterns they possess because to recognize that part of one's self would mean recognizing a need to change it.

We've all done it. But there's hope.

First, beating ourselves up over anything does no good. So if you're guilty of not dealing well with change, not seeing it coming, not learning and growing from it, fear not. It doesn't mean you can't start to deal. You see, change is inevitable, even in yourself. If we accept that change happens—that we should anticipate it and prepare for it; that we should monitor changes around us learn to adapt to change quickly, learn to actually change ourselves; that we should learn to enjoy change and welcome the fact that we must be ready to change over and over again—if we accept that, we can in fact survive it. When they move your cheese, you will have already found more, or at least have a pathway to it planned. And who knows, you might find out along the way that the goals you wanted are now not as important and others have come to the foreground. Because even our destinations can change.

The Politics of Hypocrisy

Monday night, 12:30 A.M. Just got home. Walked to a local club from my house; needed the exercise after sitting all day at the computer. During what could best be described as a mediocre strip show, the opportunity arises to go outside and smoke a joint. There, I said it. Someone wanted to go engage in the most capital of offenses, smoking a joint.

Having lived with someone who had full-blown AIDS for years, pot was commonplace in my life. Legally. My partner had a bona fide prescription. Upon his death he left two full budding plants in the backyard. So without breaking any laws at all, I found myself knee-deep in green stuff. I gave most of it away to those who needed it, but some I kept. Why not, right?

After walking down the street and casually finishing our business, I and those with me are denied access to the club. We can't be let back in—we are evil drug users who have put the bar in great jeopardy by walking down the street and smoking a joint.

Fine. They have their policies and their rights. Without any argument, away I go. Oh, away I go, that is, after I'm let back in to sign my credit card slip for the tab. Business is business, after all.

On the way home, I can't help but think of the hypocrisy of it all. Just a half hour before, the bar was happy to supply me with not one, not two, but three Absolut Mandarin rocks. Two were still lined up in front of me before I left, not being able to consume as much as friends will often buy. No questions about whether I was driving. No questions about what, if any, prescription drugs I had consumed. No questions at all. In fact, every night that's what bars do: pour out legal poison, a drug more potent than marijuana and far more responsible for an unhealthy portion of the national death toll than any joint. That is proved by statistics on both sides of the legalization issue. No one smokes too much pot and gets in a major car accident wiping out a family of four. In fact, some reports have observed that people drive more safely when high on pot than when drunk. Maybe there's something to be said for paranoia.

Any weekend at local clubs, any number of bar owners and bartenders know their patrons are on E, K, X, the designer drugs of the week. Hey, it's good for water sales. And many even partake themselves, just not in public.

On the way home, via cell phone, I am reminded that I'm a public figure and I must not enter this fray. I must not be honest about what I was doing; I must forget all about it. I should hope that word doesn't get back to my station or my good, conservative fans in Orange County. Karel, out smoking a joint. Oh, my God.

More than 10 million Vicodin tablets were consumed in America last year. Over 25 million gallons of beer and enough vodka to fill the Rose Bowl four times over. Drunk driving accidents and arrests remain dangerously high. Smoking cigarettes, which is legal, is the second-most common cause of death, and food—obesity, perfectly legal carbohydrates—is the number one cause of death, via heart disease. Get a grip, people: Marijuana is the least of our problems.

I want to call a friend and apologize for cutting his evening short with our shenanigans. Then I think better of it. Eartha Kitt told me a wonderful story once. She told me how it was illegal for a black person and a white person to share the same glass in South Africa. So at one of her shows she started champagne glasses and bottles circling about. Everyone drank after one another, white and black. There were too many people to arrest. The demonstration was successful. Eartha said, "When a law is unjust, it must be broken." A good philosophy. So no apology.

I will not hide the fact that on occasion I smoke pot, like on occasion I have a glass of wine or vodka rocks. I function. I live. I have a job. I'm a responsible person. I don't do crack, coke, heroin, E, K, X, Y, or Z. Nor do I accept the authority of a society that says it's all right to kill your liver, drink as you like, smoke tobacco (which gives its own high), get hooked on prescription drugs to make sure your mood is right, or otherwise turn to medicine at the drop of a hat for a quick fix. It's all the same. Either get rid of it all or get over it.

What I did was illegal. So was getting married in much of the country, if you were an interracial couple in the 1960s. So was voting in many states if you were black in the '50s. So is getting married now if you're a same-sex couple. Hell, so is having gay sex in more than 20 states. So was drinking alcohol at one point.

Isn't it time we get some common sense on these issues? How you choose to sedate yourself is your business, so long as you're not harming anyone or putting anyone in danger. How can we continue to say this substance is fine, this one not? (Economics, that's how, but that's another column.) In the meantime, think about it. As you stand on your antidrug moral high ground, just remember, caffeine is a potent drug, and legal at Starbucks. Alcohol is the most lethal and detrimental of almost all drugs, but it flows like water at upscale social functions and in the poorest neighborhoods. Vicodin addiction is at an all-time high (pardon the pun) and still being given out like candy by most dentists. Being self-righteous is fine, just make sure your blood is completely pure while you are.

Forty and Gay...
Impossible, You Say?

You've got to be kidding me, I thought, as I sat looking at an advertisement for a West Hollywood nightclub. *"Club 18–25"? You mean they are now doing nightclub events by age in West Hollywood? Does this speak volumes about the state of gay male culture or what? I mean, really, are they that youth- and body-obsessed that...*

As I listened to my mouth blather on—which, since my mouth belongs to a talk-show host, it is sometimes known to do—I began to wonder why I was so bothered. Was it really the unconscious politics of such a seemingly harmless thing—yet another way gay men have chosen to segregate themselves into perfect little parcels of prettiness? Or was it that I was about to turn 40 and would therefore be 15 years past getting into this party? Fact is, it was both that bothered me, and probably more of the second. What cinched this conclusion was that my 28-year-old friend Daniel was a bit miffed by the concept as well, and he could care less about social observations.

Sometimes many of us spend so much time being gay and dealing with the issues of being gay that we overlook the fact that just being human has plenty of issues—aging being top of the list. Medicine combats its effects, science searches to slow or reverse it, corporations make billions trying to conceal it, but try as we will, we can't stop the aging process. Time marches on—sometimes right across your face, leaving little tracks known to the kind of heart as "laugh lines" and to those of us wearing them as "wrinkles."

November 7, 2002, at 5:17 P.M., I turned 40. Now, I've heard all the psychobabble about how life begins at 40, the best is yet to come, so on and so forth, but all of that positive reinforcement is coming from people over 40.

Truth be told, being 40 and being gay—hell, being past 35 and being gay—isn't a picnic, and it's all men's fault. Just as Americans in general don't value aging, gay men in particular seem to have almost a phobia about older gay men. They are all but invisible in most circles and tend to school together like fish, segregating in bowling alleys and gay centers across the land. They are the placeholders at the end of a local bar or the owners of one, or the couple next door seen at the local store.

As I look at 40, I say a silent prayer to the universe: Please, universe, please don't let me become one of Them. You know who They are. They are those older gay men who refuse to let go—you know, that Lycra-wearing, I'm-going-to-pump-up-my-body-until-I-nearly-burst, gray-haired or balding guy. He still goes to circuit parties or hangs out with the much younger crowd, like the low end of the 18–25 party above. He listens to gangsta rap because it's cool. He tries very hard to stay good-looking and be accepted by all, young and old, even praised or appreciated. And while he may succeed, his effort is obvious. Yet he is completely understandable. Why? Because much like nongay women, gay men are judged by other men, and it's a man's world, men are pigs, and we gay men want to be pig fodder.

When I tell everyone my age, they don't believe it. While that's flattering, I wonder why they seem surprised. Could it be that we all have a preconceived notion of what 40 or 50 is going to be like, what we're going to be like, and how we're going to act? You bet we do, and to most of us, it's not a thought we like contemplating. Aging inherently brings out negative feelings—feelings of anxiety, fear, discontent. For those who have lived through 30, remember the feeling of urgency around such things as "needing" to own something—a house, a condo— if you didn't already, for getting that promotion, for starting that book, for settling down with a lover, for getting on with life.

But it's odd—I don't need to be made to feel good about getting older, you see, because I already do. While it's harder now to take off the weight, hangovers last for two days instead of four hours, things are hanging a little lower than before thanks to gravity, and shopping for fashionable reading glasses is a viable pastime, it's not so bad.

You see, my partner died at 34. Thirty-four years old. My dear friend Lorenzo died at 33. Countless other names, all dead before 40, some before 30. Aging in the gay community is now more a badge of honor than a number. It's almost as if instead of a party, we should get a medal, for surviving. Remember, we in our 40s came up when AIDS wasn't in the picture, watched it develop and kill, went through eras of no treatments, of uncertainty. If you're over 40 and gay, you're a survivor, a testament to either Western medicine or careful decision-making. And you lived through disco, its resurgence, punk, and '80s rock. That alone deserves something.

Sure, I hang around younger people. One of my best friends, Young Jason, is 27. That's 13 years my junior. Yet he's a godsend. And just as he keeps me youthful, I'd like to think I do the same for another of my friends who just turned 57 but acts 37. There is no age barrier to friendship (within reason of course, people). And since that is one of the most important things in the world, well, turning 40 doesn't seem so terrible.

It is sad that most 40-plus gay men don't make more of a presence in mainstream social circles. Maybe aging gays are coupled or are too busy with jobs and lives to be out and about. Maybe they fear the same age prejudices that women face. Or maybe they fall asleep right after *The West Wing*.

So somewhere between the psychobabble and harsh realities lies the truth, the truth that aging isn't the curse many think but the blessing many miss. I wouldn't want to be 20 right now if you paid me. While the skin may be much tighter, I like the wisdom and comfort that come with age. And while it's harder to find a date, it's easier to find parking thanks to the handicapped placard secured for that trick knee blown out during the gymnastic days of breakdancing or injured kneeling at the bathhouses in the late '70s.

The self-esteem of gay men often takes a beating—after all, society barely accepts us, and even in our own community we segregate—but aging shouldn't eat at it. We've survived AIDS, the Reagan administration, and two Bushes (so far). We've learned enough about love to save us time on worthless pursuits and seen enough to help some younger people avoid our same mistakes. Life doesn't begin at 40 for a gay man, but it certainly doesn't end. Maybe there should be a 35–50 night at some establishment. On the other hand, something tells me that Club 18–25 will turn into Club 18–50, because let's face it, there are always more than a few silver foxes around a henhouse.

Just a Simple Block of Text

It's amazing, the little things in life that can take your breath away. You know, that something that comes from out of the blue and hits like a freight train at full speed, completely unexpected. It could be anything, from a phone call from a past love to a simple little block of text.

It was simple enough. The doorbell rang, and there was my dependable UPS man standing with yet another package. Given my line of work, I receive quite a few, so we're on a first-name basis. What's this? A box from the attorney who's handling the wrongful-death suit for me? Yes, I'm a same-sex domestic partner in the state of California filing a civil suit against the people I believe are responsible for the wrongful death of my late partner. Sharon Smith made headlines suing the people responsible for the dogs who killed Diane Alexis Smith, her partner; I'm suing the hospital and doctors who I believe let my partner, Andrew, die in an emergency room on Pride weekend without giving him the proper treatment that could have saved his life.

OK, so this is more paperwork. A lawsuit takes a lot of paperwork.

I open the box. There, on the top, is a document I haven't seen in almost a year—Andrew's death certificate, that horrendous piece of paper that makes the past 14 months so very real. My name is on it too. In the space used to designate where "the remains shall be remanded," there is my name. But right below it, it has a place for "Spouse's Name." That box is empty. Completely, totally, mockingly empty. My name does not appear in there.

Wham!

Then there's the "coroner's report," right below it. Within the coroner's remarks is a place for statements. I, of course, had been interviewed by the police and coroner when Andrew died (due to his sudden death). In that paragraph, that block of text, it says "The decedent's friend of 12 years." *Friend.* When it's all said and done, there I am, not listed in the spouse box and labeled his "friend of 12 years."

Wham! Bam!

Recently I have written columns calling our activists' strategies into question. I have been a dissenting voice in the gay community, both on radio and in print. But make no mistake, I realize how now, more than ever, we need activists. We need visibility. We need change. From the simplest of things, like Los Angeles County changing their forms to reflect the legality of domestic partnerships in this state—a simple typesetting change—to shifting the prevalent attitude in this country about the invalidity of same-sex relationships.

How we effect this change is up for debate, but without a doubt, we've got a long way to go to achieve it. Reminders are all around us. Those subtle jabs, the not-so-subtle assaults, the things that happen quickly and feel like concrete blocks being hurled at our chests. Those empty text blocks. We've each had them. The mother who finds out that one of her sons is looking at bondage porn, and while relaying this to her gay son—the gay son who has helped support her, loved her, been there for her—she says "Well, at least he's not gay..." (Yes, a true story; it happened to a close friend of mine.) Or finding out that the neighbor who loves and adores you, comes over, visits, sits with you and your partner in the backyard, talking about how unfair it is the way gay people are treated—that neighbor has turned around and voted for a law to keep marriage restricted to unions between a man and a woman because, well, that is the way God intended...yet another true story right from my neighborhood.

Reminders. Reminders that for all the ground we've covered, all the battles we've fought, all the parades we've marched in, it's the simplest of things, those little text blocks, those little comments that can move us ahead or set us back so far.

So to those who may read my writings and think I've gone too far to the right, to those who think a dissenting voice is wrong at time when we need unity, to those who believe to question is to disapprove, know this: I'm there with you each and every step of the way. I too feel the bigotry of the main-stream even though I am a part of it. I too get those bricks hurled and sometimes don't have the strength to throw any back. And, I too wait for someone to help make it better. And then realize it's up to me to do just that.

Slightly Off Center

The road to hell is truly paved with good intentions, and it would appear that one of the off-ramps of that well-traversed highway leads to the countless gay and lesbian community service centers across the country. Nowhere will you find more well-intentioned volunteers and employees, board members, and trustees than at these centers; and nowhere will you find a group of more talented people absolutely out of touch with the community that they allegedly serve, a group almost as self-serving as the politicians they often pander to and the corporations they seek out for money.

I have been out, and in the community, for almost 25 years, and along the way have had dealings with the centers that "serve" me—and each time walked away shaking my head in disbelief. I have talked to many board members of various organizations over the years, each group with its own internal horror story. I have watched as the community outgrew and outpaced the efforts of those that would represent us. I have read of scandal after scandal at various organizations—resignations, replacements, regaling.

Signs of it are all around. Literally. While getting afternoon tea one day I happened upon a container, a very "Jerry's Kids"–looking receptacle. But this wasn't for a particular disease it was a plea to help the local gay and lesbian center collect $25,000 to pay off back taxes. How on earth did any well-run million-dollar organization get $25,000 in debt with the IRS? The answer isn't even germane; the fact that it happened is.

Another glaring sign was revealed to me when I realized that political infighting and personal gain play into the politics of any center. Case in point: A local center had a huge benefit planned...large ad campaign, high visibility, a very noble and, for all intents and purposes, fun event destined to bring together many members of the community—all in all, a great goal from which everyone benefited. Of course, there was more than a little "off-the-record" grumbling from the organizing committee when it was revealed that one of the event's organizers was throwing a competing event, one block away and for the same price—advertised as the "official" event for the evening. It was a private function, with the proceeds going into the local bar owner's pocket.

Obviously, someone was optimistic that there was enough pie to vivisect into a million little pieces and have everyone win. While both events may have been successes in their own right, what a blaring conflict of interest, and to an outsider, it would almost appear as sabotage. How committed to the success of the center's event really was the organizer of that second party—who was supposedly a pillar of the center? What message did it send to the entire community?

One reading is this: The center is for *those* people, and we have to support it to be good gays and lesbians. But for *us*, the real party is elsewhere. When we're done with the tiresome duty of supporting the center, we will return to our regularly scheduled lives, in which the center plays no part.

When a good friend and I first moved to our community, I called our local gay and lesbian center to see if it could help him manage his HIV. I was told no new clients were being accepted because the center was $60,000 short and couldn't afford another case manager. We reached out, our hand was slapped. We were referred to a local hospital that had an AIDS outreach program, which proved futile as well. Ultimately, we ended up doing research on the Web and through friends to get the necessary information and find him the proper health care.

I would like to believe that it's just me who wonders what real role gay and lesbian centers are playing in most gays' and lesbians' lives. But I individually polled hundreds of people from all age groups and demographics, in bars, coffeehouses, dinner parties, in print, on the air—any place a group of diverse gay and lesbian people gathered. I asked: Has your local gay center impacted your life in any way that you are aware? Do you feel it's relevant to you and your lifestyle? Do you have any idea what functions it does, how and why? When is the last time you contacted it or were involved in one of its events or programs? (Attending center benefits doesn't count.)

Most of the people I talked to were clueless, uninvolved, or had some association that proved futile. Many didn't even know where their center was located or what services it offered.

Now, this apathy toward gay and lesbian centers isn't surprising in a nation where only a miniscule number of people eligible to vote actually do so and in a community like ours that covers so many age groups, so much ethnic and financial diversity. Nonetheless it's a telling tale. And what's worse, many of those who did voice opinions thought these places were in self-repeating cycles, raising money to keep themselves going to raise more money, or to give money to other organizations just as disjointed or consumed by internal politics as themselves. They throw benefits to pat themselves on the back or to honor those who donate. They honor politicians and community leaders who are involved in their dealings, rarely being controversial or groundbreaking.

Now, these are vast generalizations to say the least, and certainly the data is not scientific. But there is a truth underlying it all: Our centers have not adjusted to our needs. They are not the "centers" of our community but operate somewhere on the outskirts of it. Yes, they do good work, and yes, they are needed. When my late husband, Andrew, found out about his HIV, his mother didn't know what to do, so she drove him to the local gay center. Here is an excerpt from our book, *Guarded Optimism*. This passage was written by Andrew himself, and it speaks volumes.

"I felt like the freak of the week as my mother and brother decided that they must drive me down the hill to the Gay and Lesbian Community Service Center of Orange County. It was time to call in reinforcements, and, since they had no clue about my lifestyle, they thought they'd bring me to the experts.

"I must say, that in spite of my objections to them bringing me, it did seem like a bright light at the end of a very dark tunnel. Normally, I don't think the centers really get much done. They had not adversely or positively affected my life in any way, or those around me, in the gay community. At least not that I could see. I viewed them as organizations set up to give people something to do without really doing something. None of their programs really seemed to touch my life.

"Now, however, I was grateful for their existence.

"When we arrived and my mother blurted to the volunteer behind the desk that her son had just been diagnosed with HIV the volunteer immediately called in their HIV program coordinator. He knew exactly what to do—nothing.

" 'We're sorry, there really is no known cure or many treatments right now. However, there is a program at the Orange County Health Department for those with HIV. It's very new and very crowded, but I will give you a referral...'

"Happy, happy, joy, joy. My shining beacon became a smoldering ember."

Not the help they were looking for, but help nonetheless. Yes, a sense of community is important for our gay and lesbian youth, and for those who find their centers, it can be their first step toward finding themselves. Beyond that, to many, the role of the gay and lesbian center is a mystery.

Perhaps that's why so many centers struggle financially. People in the community are hesitant to give simply out of obligation—today, it's all about bang for the buck. So what's to be done?

Many, myself included, feel these groups shouldn't be the centers of the community, but that they should work their way into it and become its very fabric. Innovative marketing must be used to get quality people from all areas involved. And their boards and leaders must disregard the muck they seem mired in and not be afraid to ruffle feathers, even the feathers of those on their boards or in their executive offices. More importantly, each needs a strong leader—because not everything should be or is best done by committee. Leaders of gay centers must do just that: lead the organization in this new millennium, adopting new attitudes and disregarding the often antiquated ideals of their predecessors.

As many gays and lesbians move beyond "gay" and incorporate themselves and their families into the mainstream, the centers need to do the same. Their jobs should be that of ambassadors, of chambers of commerce, of political action committees. Much as groups like the National Association for the Advancement of Colored People have come under fire from members of the community it serves for not modernizing its infrastructure and methodology, our centers should listen more and object less. Stop infighting and start doing more.

And focus. Remember, serving us is one thing, but aren't we better served by bridging the gap between our community and our nongay counterparts? Shouldn't a center's first focus be exposing our culture to those who don't understand it, in an effort to bring about tolerance?

Part of the problem is that it's easier for those in the community to simply opt out than to question, to criticize, to effect change. Those inside these organizations who challenge the status quo are often dismissed or disparaged (à la Larry Kramer). Many who speak up (or out) find that their cries fall on deaf ears. Those in the community who speak out publicly are seen as turncoats. And here we sit in 2002 with many centers scrambling to pay the rent and keep the lights on and many feeling they wouldn't miss them if the lights went off. And truth be told, many wouldn't.

OK, I hear you say, if I'm such a hotbed of ideas, why not sign up and effect change myself? For the very reasons I've stated. I've sat in board meetings and found myself wishing the ceiling would collapse and a beam fall on me to put me out of my misery. I've listened as the ideas came and went, with the deciding factor on many policies being not what was being suggested but who was suggesting it. I've met with leaders and offered ideas, only to have been told why they can't be done: don't have the money, too much to handle, don't have the manpower, too controversial, not enough internal support—I've heard it all. Quite frankly, it appears I can shape more opinion and get more done in a broadcast studio or at my TiBook than I can in a boardroom.

Our centers and our "leaders" need to do just that. They need to re-center themselves—refocus and come out with a clearer picture of what we really need instead of what it is they're used to doing. Stop using lack of funding for an excuse and find, through modernization, that funding will come as involvement increases. And beyond all that, stop playing personality games with each other—cut the crap. Remove the petty politics and deal with the matters at hand. There are good role models out there, centers that get the job done. Find those and get a model, a pattern. Take the best of the best and merge it with homegrown innovation. *Make* me, us, the community care. *Make* us know who you are and what you do. *Make* us feel you're relevant.

Most involved with these organizations want that very thing, and many know how to achieve it. Let them be heard, let them lead. We need many voices—give us another one, a louder one, a focused one, a *central*ized one.

Romance Is
Where You Find It

My late husband Andrew hated Valentine's Day. He just hated being told he "had" to tell someone he loved them because greeting card companies and candy makers said so. He wasn't romantic in that sense. I, on the other hand, am a hopeful romantic, believing in the magic of moonlit walks, flowers, holding hands in the park.

Yet each February 14 I awoke to flowers or a card, breakfast in bed, something nice. He gave in, for me, hating it all the while but doing it nonetheless. And, as I approach this February 14 alone, I realize romance is where you find it, it's in the details.

You see, even though Andrew wasn't a romantic, he recognized the importance of it. For my birthday once, he gave me the gift of romance. He was great at gifts, always doing themes. This year it was to be romance. When I awoke he blindfolded me. Drove me to the train station. He had secured our own compartment. We got on a train bound for San Francisco. In the compartment were my things and my computer. When I went to get wine, he plugged in the DVD of *The American President,* my favorite romantic film. Once in San Francisco at the Hyatt Regency Embarcadero, at midnight he handed me a small box. Inside was a gold band. I was thrilled. He said, "Not for you, silly, for me," and held out his hand. You see, he didn't wear jewelry, and for 10 years I had asked him to wear a ring. Now he let me slide one on his finger. Then he gave me a bigger box, with paperwork. It was my ring, a carat and a half, that he designed, and he slid it on my finger. A more romantic night, or birthday, one could not hope to have.

Since his death I have had the pleasure of two very romantic moments: one, with Young Jason, high atop the Sky Room in Long Beach. Candlelit dinner, romantic music, the chef bringing us his latest creations while the manager handled the wine, followed by a rooftop stroll, holding hands, drinking cosmopolitans high above the city. We came home, danced in my empty TV room to Michael Jackson videos, hugged.

The next was with Daniel A., at the Hotel Palomar in San Francisco. There we sat, in the Magritte Suite, Jacuzzi filled with warm water and bubbles. Candles burning. Emma Shapplin's Popera album *Etterna* playing on my iPod over portable speakers, wine. We laughed, we blew bubbles at each other, we chatted as we Jacuzzied in a posh hotel during a San Francisco rainstorm. Romance was definitely in the air.

Yet, notice what *didn't* happen in those two moments—sex, because while romance is definitely part of sex, it is not exclusive to it. You don't need one to have the other; in fact, sex can often ruin a very romantic moment.

There are those who believe romance is dead in the gay community. I disagree. I've felt it, experienced it firsthand. It's just that gay men, or men in general, seem hardwired to believe that these moments must end in orgasm or they're simply not worth it. Balderdash. They are so worth it, they are what you remember, they are the stuff of which dreams are made. In fact, sex without romance is worthless, meaningless, a mere body function. I'll take one train ride, one Sky Room, one Hotel Palomar over a hundred meaningless orgasms.

Valentine's Day can make those who are alone feel even more so. To them I say, grab romance where you can—with a friend, an intimate, someone special. Don't negate the power of a simple moment, even if that moment isn't sexual. Connect in some romantic way and accept that as enough, because believe me, it can be; it is.

And to gay men, how about letting through some of the "feminine" side we're so often stereotyped as having? Romantic dinners aren't drive-throughs after the bars close, on the way home to boff, or buying Naya water for the group of hotties at the circuit party before running back to the hotel room. How about remembering that romance is connection, and *that*, more than sex, is what most people need and want. Sure, sex can be a part of it, but it doesn't have to *be* it. Let your heart live a little—one day you'll hold those moments so precious, so dear. What happens in the bedroom can often fade out of memory; what happens before is what remains.

Know When to
Hold 'Em

It was an ordinary Tuesday evening. That's what should have scared me.

It started fine. My roommate and I watched one of our favorite shows, BBC America's *Ground Force*. They were in New York, redoing a garden for Bette Midler's nonprofit, no less. Great fun. The night was young. We decided to go out.

We arrived at the Brit. Lance Todd, the bartender, is a good friend and talented musician, so we decided to stop in, say hello, and hear if he had any new songs to play us. His mood was heavy.

"Did you hear?" he asked. I knew what he was talking about. Two local talk-show hosts on my old station decided to bash me on the previous Friday. That's nothing new, they always do. But this time it got personal. Seems I said stuff on CNN's *Talkback Live* they didn't like. I never mentioned their names, but they did mine.

"I can't even repeat what they said—because I'm your friend. I can't even say it," he went on. I knew already.

Many fans had e-mailed me. I didn't hear their show; I was out of town.

I asked Lance if it changed his opinion of me. He said no. I asked my roommate if he still wanted to live with me. He said yes. I then assured them both that no matter what they said, it couldn't matter that much if everyone around me who loved me still did.

We bid goodbye to Lance and went to the Mine Shaft. I don't normally frequent that bar. But Tuesday is "their" night in Long Beach, the place where most people go. I had great conversations with friends who stopped by. Then, near the end of the evening, someone playing pool stepped on my exposed toes in their Doc Martens boots and stayed there. I moved his foot, and told him it was OK that he destroyed those five, I had five more. He turned and hit me in the face with the pool cue. He split my lip. Blood flew. When I asked him what the hell he was doing, he hit me again. Everyone stood in disbelief. And I did nothing except ask for the bouncer to have him removed and sit bleeding.

Three days earlier I was in San Francisco, on the number one talk station there, KGO, debating with a member of the NAACP about whether the first black police chief of San Francisco should have made a big deal about someone delivering watermelons to City Hall. I questioned him about picking battles wisely when attacked.

I was attacked twice in one week. Once on the air and once in the flesh. And I chose not to fight back in any major way. I turned the other cheek. Am I happy about it? No. I would love to sue the asses off those hosts, but in radio you're signing your own death warrant if you sue a station or hosts for slander. And I like to work. I like to be one of the few openly gay people working in radio. And as for the bar incident, well, you lie down with dogs, you'll get fleas. I'm not about to start a barroom brawl, even in self-defense, because given the anger I feel over so many things, from the loss of my husband to being attacked on the air, I may not have stopped. And involuntary manslaughter is still a crime.

I sat thinking about all of this. Crying a little, asking my late husband what he would have done. And it became clearer to me than ever before. I am a big analogy. I am what I argued about with the guy from the NAACP. I am what's wrong with the gay community.

You see, we carry so much baggage. We've been attacked so many times. So when someone does it now, we fight back, in a big, vocal way. Even if the higher ground, as in the case of the San Francisco police chief, is to laugh it off. We can't let go. Because we've been wronged so badly, so many times.

Do I want to hurt the guy who hit me? Sure. Do I want those radio hosts to fail? Yup. Do I understand any of it? Nope. I mean, why do they hate me? I know one of the radio hosts hates that Andrew and I came from nowhere while he worked crap jobs for years. As for the guy in the bar, he was drunk.

But history tells me to choose my battles wisely. Live to fight another day. And choose your battles well.

Not everything deserves the effort. I'm a big boy. I can take a hit in the face. My lip will heal, my black eye will mend, and the bar gets a great story to tell. Karel, socked in the bar. KFI listeners get to decide whether the talk-show hosts crossed the line by tuning them out or continuing to listen. The NAACP gets to decide whether to laugh off a racial incident. So how about us in the gay community as a whole lightening up a little too?

You see, I know that not everyone is like those hosts, like the fool that sent the watermelon, like the guy who hit me. I know they are a minority. I also know that all the anger I may bring to one of those fights won't help me win the battle. That's what we must learn as gay people.

We have been wronged. Matthew Shepard died. Billy Jack Gaither, so many others. No, we can't marry, and no, we're not equal yet. But bringing all that anger to the table won't help us now. That anger, that righteous indignation will only cloud what we do and how we do it. There is a bigger, better goal, and we must let go of the past to get to it. I never had a slave, and many around us have never discriminated against a gay person. Let's not blame the sins of the past on every person in our present.

I've had to say goodbye to so much in the past 15 months. My husband, my job, my life as I knew it. As a public figure, I have to know what it's like to be beaten up, either in the press or in real life. And I know that as long as I live to fight another battle, earning respect for taking the high road along the way, I'll win, even if at times I feel as though all is lost. I'll fight back when I need to, and when I can, on the issues at hand and not on the issues of the past. And I'll realize that not every strike deserves one back. Some can be chalked up to experience.

So lighten up. Turn the other cheek. Leave the Louis Vuitton behind. When you go to bat for us, leaders, don't bring up the past, think about the future. Do what you must to win the war, not the battle. And stop fighting the small stuff. Our wounds are deep, but they will heal. Let's work on preventing new ones. Know when to demand more, when to fight harder, and when to say, "You know what? It's fine. Things aren't great, but the greater good was served."

Am I saying lie down? Nope. I'm simply saying we all must learn when to hold 'em and how to win without folding.

You see, I win if I keep working, giving the community a voice. I win if I'm not in jail for beating an idiot to near death. As a community, we win if we can argue the current issues, not the abuses of the past. Don't blame me for the minstrel shows and I won't blame you for Stonewall. Don't rehash what was, let's talk about what is. If someone sends you a melon, slice it up and eat it. If someone bashes you at work, do what you must to ensure you will succeed further and in spite of them. If someone tries to unleash your anger upon them by striking you, be sure you won't gain more by walking away before you decide to strike back. Respect is not something you can demand; it must be earned. How you gain it is up to you. And how we gain it as a community is up to us. If we blame society forever for all its sins, then we'll never be able to work with it to ensure our future. But if we learn that sometimes the best way to strike back is to not strike at all, to make it a nonissue, then we could end up with what we want after all.

Ray of Light

Ray is tall. Ray has red hair. Ray is an athlete. Ray is drop-dead gorgeous. Ray is sweet. Ray always has a kind word. Ray is a bartender in a gay bar. And Ray is straight.

I never really thought about the last part, Ray being straight—well, any more than any gay man thinks about a gorgeous straight man: "What a shame, but he'll make beautiful babies and one of those might be gay, so that's OK. I mean, we've got to replenish our supply somehow, don't we?" But one night, out with my friends, a rather drunken compadre felt a need to tell Ray he had no right to be working in a gay bar, making money off of gay men all drooling over him, if he was unavailable to them, if he wasn't one of them.

Was this a case of *in vino veritas* (in wine lies truth) or just the ramblings of a drunken mess? I couldn't dismiss the complaint because it is one I have voiced in other situations. But as I sat apologizing to Ray for my friend's actions, it all became very clear to me.

You see, for years I've made a good living off of heterosexuals. In radio I was the only gay person on the station, talking to a large audience of nongays. In acting I've played the role of a heterosexual (that's why it's called *acting*) in heterosexual productions and plays. I've worked for nongay companies, ones with no other gay employees. Should I not have been allowed? Should nongays only hire their own, and gays do the same?

Poppycock.

It's been an issue in Hollywood for years—straight actors playing gay characters. In *Queer as Folk* several leads are not gay (or so they say). Should they not be allowed? Since there are so few roles for gays and lesbians, do the producers owe it to the community to hire from within? Nope, they owe it to the part to pick the best actor, gay or otherwise, as long as they are not excluding gay actors from the running. Should gay and lesbian publications not employ nongay writers, printers, photographers? Of course not. Some of my dearest friends in journalism are not gay, and many write for the gay media. Are they taking a job away from a good gay journalist? No more than anyone else deprives someone of a job by filling it.

It all boils down to honesty for me. For instance, Ray does not hide his sexuality. Nor does he "tease" his clients, offering them false hope. Brandon, another nongay bartender working at a gay club, is another fine example. He's a great guy making a living and having fun. No dishonesty. Can gays say the same?

Case in point: In a recent *Out* magazine article the new actor from *Queer as Folk,* who plays the HIV-positive love interest of Michael (Hal Sparks), was asked if he was gay. I won't say his name, for reasons I'll explain in a moment. He was quoted as saying he didn't think the answer to the question would help the show or his character, so he'd like to leave it unanswered for now. Well, he has that right. But *Out* should have pulled the story. I'm sorry, if you're making money playing a gay character, getting a full layout in a gay magazine, you can at least be honest about your sexuality. If not, that's your choice, but we shouldn't promote this guy. Call us when you can be honest.

Of course, he did just that—called when he could be honest. He called *The Advocate* and came out a few months after the *Out* interview. Good for him, so why the delay?

But the problem is, we are guilty of reverse discrimination. Many gay and lesbians want to be exclusive in their business practices. Yes, we win the battle by empowering our own, by giving those in the community a leg up through the financial support of employment. But does it have to be all or nothing? And would we want our nongay counterparts to do the same? If a gay man wants to bartend at Yankee Doodles or Live Bait (please, God, first tell me why), shouldn't they be allowed? They'd sue if they were denied the job. The American Civil Liberties Union would rally. Well, who rallies for the countless nongays who are turned away by gay businesses strictly because they're not "one of us"? Oh, that's not the reason they're given, but bet your Streisand collection it's the underlying reason.

I say we win the battle through people like Ray, Brandon, and the countless other nongay people who chose to live and work in our community; people who have moved beyond sexuality and truly are about integration. If these people were homophobic in their lives then no, we shouldn't support them. But I haven't met too many homophobic nongays working in any predominantly gay business, from bars to publications, restaurants to movie studios. No, these people work in our community, become our friends, socialize with us outside of the clubs with their girlfriends, or boyfriends in the female nongay scenario. And we win. We win because to them, we're normal, everyday, commonplace. They are more likely to support pro-gay legislation, more likely to be our champions with some of their friends who may not be as supportive. We gain not only a good employee but an ambassador, an advocate.

Balance is what we need in this situation. Yes, we must continue to support our own. I've always had a problem with gay magazines that constantly put nongays on the cover. Covers are hard to get, so when they are available on our own magazines, let's give them to those in the community who need or warrant the attention. But not exclusively—we can promote a few nongays as well in those cases. And in our businesses we have room for both gay and nongay employees. If we want people to believe we have room in the world for both gay and nongay people, it should apply all the way down to our establishments, our bars. There really is room, everywhere, for everybody who is honest, sincere, and concerned with getting the job done, and not the sexuality of the person doing it.

A B-a-a-a-a-a-h-d Idea

Birds do it, bees do it, even educated fleas do it—now add sheep to that list. What is it? Gay sex, of course. Scientists have long observed homosexual behavior in all areas of the animal kingdom, not just among humans. Barbara Walters once did a special about lesbian seagulls in California's Santa Monica Bay. There have been gay chimps—hell, even beetles (no, not Ringo, although I always did wonder).

Now scientists have announced there are gay rams—indeed, male sheep so gay that they never even sniff around the females. They're gay, gay, gay. And the world has taken note: For over six days it was the number one story e-mailed by people visiting ABCnews.com. I know I got it in my in-box. Everyone was fascinated with the fact that rams were getting it on with other rams.

Now, why anyone outside the state of Arkansas would even care about the love life of sheep is beyond me, but there it was. The rams, they said, would help scientists to understand humans and give them insight into the biological aspects of homosexuality. It would help them find out what makes sheep, and eventually people, gay.

Danger, Will Robinson! Danger!

I have never been comfortable with the idea of finding out what genetic code makes me or anyone else gay. When researcher Simon Levay felt a need to dissect the brains of men who had died from HIV to see if there was some abnormality, some genetic clue, I wasn't cheering him on—just as I wish the scientists studying those swinging rams would leave well enough alone.

Why? Well, there's a wonderful line in *Jurassic Park* that applies (if I may paraphrase): We're so busy figuring out if we could, we don't stop to think about if we should. You see, no one, no matter how noble, looks for information simply for information's sake. There's always an end, an agenda. Much of modern-day anthropology was rooted in the quest to prove the white man superior to the black man by studying of the cranium, lobes, development, etc. Don't think for a minute that there aren't those who want the "root" of homosexuality found so they can "fix" or "cure" it.

If the genetic makeup of homosexuality is discovered, you bet your booties someone will find a way to test unborn children for it, then alter or abort based on the information. Science fiction? Hardly. Designer babies are already here, and if some young mother was told her child was going to be gay, believe me, many would try to change it or stop it from happening.

This research only plays into the thinking that homosexuality is a disease, a genetic fluke—to quote my dear friend Dr. Laura, "a biological error." Why were queers so upset at her for that when scientists are out there trying to prove just that very thing? "Oh, if people see that we can't help it, that it's biological, it will help us, we will be seen as 'normal' then," I hear from those around me. Poppycock. Humans love to look at, segregate, and stigmatize biological oddities. Proving the roots of homosexuality to be biological would not spur progress for our movement or win us new acceptance; on the contrary, it would give those who call us "freaks" more ammunition.

I for one don't care what makes me gay. I just love the fact that I am.

How blessed I've been to be able to live outside the confines of the "traditional" male. How wondrous it was to love a man like I loved my Andrew; how honored I was to have him. I don't wake up and question what makes me have better fashion sense, an eye for design, or the need to seek comfort in the arms of another man. And neither should anyone else.

We need to move beyond that. Acceptance won't come once a cause is found—not if it hasn't been forthcoming already. We have to move beyond the "why" to the "is." We are gay; who really cares why? Do heterosexuals wonder each day what makes them that way? Do they pour millions of dollars into research to figure it out? They should. After all, they're responsible for most of the overpopulation of the world, most of the domestic abuse, most of the child abuse— indeed, it's mathematically certain that the majority of the world's problems are caused by heterosexuals. Perhaps they should genetically control that.

And what of other research? Why not examine what clicks on inside the brain to make people believe in unsubstantiated stories as fact, chemistry that creates such a zeal for a mythical figure that people are willing to fly into buildings or wage war in the name of something they have created in their own minds? What chemistry goes astray in the brain that tells people to hate—that it's OK to beat someone and tie them to a fence post; to create second-class citizens because they're not like themselves? Let's get to the biological root of hatred or religious fanaticism, since a human body is simply chemical reactions just waiting to be explained. There are a lot more harmful things one can be other than gay; let's keep our scientists busy unraveling those mysteries and leave something as basic as sexuality alone.

Truth be told, perhaps all of us would like to know the root of gayness on some level. But the problem is the world in general wouldn't know what to do with the information. We don't live in Shangri-la, in an ideal world. We live in a world where those who are different are often disparaged, persecuted, and killed, regardless of the cause. During the days of slavery and well into the 1960s no one cared why people were black, about the melanin of the skin, nothing—all they cared about was that they were different and thus not equal.

Information such as the root of sexuality has no place in our world; we're not ready for it. History bears this out.

To the scientists I say, "Don't fix me, I'm not broken." I'm not in need of a cure. I don't care why my eyes are green, why my skin is white, or why I like to sleep with men. Some things I can accept as fact, as normal. And that's the real problem here. The motive here is to prove gay people are abnormal, bottom line. Granted, we are. We are in fact a biological abnormality, simply meaning that we're different from the rest. That is a fact; knowing why won't change the fact, won't help it, won't do anything except provide an avenue down which more bigotry will pass, more segregation will occur, and the "us" and "them" ideology will be further entrenched.

So rams have sex with each other. So what? So I have sex with another man. So what? You want to know why? Because nature intended that it be so. When we grow up as a race, as a culture, we can know more. Until that distant future, some things are better left a mystery.

•

Months after I wrote this I received the following e-mail. The next-to-last paragraph only assures me that this kind of research would be used for *exactly* the purpose I stated in the column: to do away with gays and lesbians, either out of "concern" for the life of the child or bigotry.

From: Michael George
Date: Wed Mar 19, 2003 8:55:25 PM US/Pacific
To: comments@karelchannel.com
Subject: We, like sheep Comment

Hi,

I am a college student doing some research into sexual orientation specifically in K–12 schools. I stumbled across the sheep in Idaho and then onto your article.

In your article you question why anyone who was gay might want to be something else. I think I have an answer.

In my research I have found that gays, lesbians, and bi-sexuals (GLB's) have suicidal thoughts in adolescence in the range of 50%–70% and actual suicide attempt rates that range from 30% to 42%.

GLB's especially males are victimized in high school with verbal abuse, threats of violence, violence, and threatened with weapons and exposure.

GLB's are often forced to leave home when they tell their families they are gay, especially males.

GLB's have difficulty in life with identity foreclosure due to lack of role models.

Gay men still suffer high instances of HIV due to unprotected sex.

The religious right and GLB groups waste millions each year each trying to advance agendas. Each is trying to control the public school so they can inject or block agendas based on their leanings.

You might argue that these are not the problems of GLB's and the problems of society and the religious right. You might be correct with the argument that the world needs to be less cruel toward minorities, however the reality is that growing up gay is tough. Based on my research if I knew an unborn was going to be gay and I knew that his/her orientation could be changed with drugs/hormones during development, I

believe based on the current state of the world and our society that the correct choice would be to spare the child from
victimization of his/her sexual orientation, especially if the
child was male.

This is just my opinion and you can take it for what it's
worth. However, you asked the question and for comments.

Take care,
Michael

A Death in Newark

Eddie "Gwen" Araujo is dead at 17. It's tragic—yet another case plucked from the headlines, a story forged in bigotry and hatred nurtured in the small town of Newark, Calif. Araujo, by all accounts, was a sweet guy—kind, gentle, well-liked. Not the kind of person who should end up beaten nearly to death, then strangled and buried in a shallow grave.

So how did 17-year-old Araujo end up with such a fate? Through ignorant acts of violence, a comic series of cataclysmic events that were destined to end poorly—events that shouldn't happen in a perfect world but do—events that have happened before and yet we have chosen to ignore.

Araujo was a boy, biologically. However, he chose to live and dress as a woman. This takes courage in a town like Newark, particularly at that age. Kids are cruel from the start, let alone young adults with hormones raging and attitudes flaring.

Araujo was at a party with schoolmates, schoolmates from whom he obviously had a big secret—cataclysmic event number one. I guess no one had ever shown Araujo, his friends, or family the Brandon Teena story, in which a young girl gets beaten and killed by her supposed friends for hiding and lying about her true sex. I suppose no counselor, parent, or confidant had told Araujo that we don't live in a perfect world, and that there are those who would do him harm just because he is different, and that like it or not he must choose his friends, and social circles, very carefully. It would appear that no one mentioned to him in detail that living an illusion means that you have to be very careful who you fool and why. If someone did tell him this, if they tried, then the message didn't get through.

We've seen this scenario lead to a horrible end in real life with Brandon and in countless bad TV movies and films: The girl's really a guy and other guys freak out. I can't help but think someone should have seen this coming, a disaster waiting to happen.

So there sits Araujo, at a party, when his sexuality is called into question. He sits silently—all of this according to Nicole Brown, a partygoer quoted in the *Los Angeles Times* (October 22, 2002). Then this Brown girl "encourages" the others to find out. So Michael Magidson, 22 (what is a 22-year-old doing at a party with 17-year-olds?) and Araujo go into the bathroom to find out—cataclysmic event number two. I can't imagine what made Araujo enter the bathroom of his own free will. Was he forced? Did he know then that he was in danger? Were the rumors of him engaging in sexual acts with partygoers true?

Whatever the case, while in there, according to Brown, people at the party begin relaying to Brown sexual experiences they allegedly had with Araujo. To date this has not been verified, but one can only imagine that a sexually active transvestite in Newark would have been hard to keep a secret.

After about half an hour (again, according to Brown) she goes into the bathroom to see what's up. She sees Araujo sitting on the sink. She opens Araujo's legs and leaves the bathroom shouting Araujo's business to the world—cataclysmic event number three.

Next thing, according to Brown, Magidson is wrestling Araujo to the ground. That's all she recalls, because after causing such a stir, basically destroying Araujo's veil of secrecy, she, of course, casually takes off to another destination.

What happened next to Araujo is still a mystery. Magidson and two others, Jaron Nabors and Jose Merel, have been charged with Araujo's murder, after Nabors confessed and led police to Araujo's body buried in a shallow grave 150 miles east of Newark in the Sierra Nevada foothills. Why no charges have been brought against Brown is still a mystery to me. After all, she's the one who bellowed out "Oh, my God, it's a man!"—or, loosely translated to a group of straight guys who probably were having sexual thoughts about Araujo and who now realized they were fantasizing about a man, "Let the games begin!"

Now the three men have been charged with murder with a hate-crime enhancement. A hate-crime enhancement? I suppose Araujo would be less dead if they had killed him because he said something they didn't like, or cheated on one of them, or one of a million other reasons used by killers to explain their actions. I assume the parents of another 17-year-old killed merely for wearing gang colors by accident in the wrong neighborhood don't want the same punishment for the killers of their child that the Araujos do for theirs. Somehow these boys killing Araujo for being a transvestite is more horrific and carries more of a sentence than if they had beaten and strangled him for some other reason.

Poppycock.

Michael Magidson, Jaron Nabors, and Jose Merel should be prosecuted to the fullest extent of the law if they are guilty because they beat, strangled and killed another human, regardless of whether they called him "fag" or "jew" or "nigger" before they did it, regardless of whether they beat him for hiding his gender or for taking their car keys. Murder is murder, dead is dead, and the phrase *hate crime* is a redundancy. When someone is about to kill you, they're not doing it with love and compassion in their hearts. At that moment, they hate you enough to do away with you, and as someone who's been held at gunpoint, trust me, you don't really care why, you just want it to end without getting killed.

It's safe to assume that Araujo didn't care why they were tying the rope around his neck; he simply wanted someone to help him, to make them stop. Actions, not motivations, are what's important to the person being attacked. Hate crime laws are just another way to create a class of victims, people who need special care and protection under the law because existing laws just don't seem good enough. Yet existing laws already work: They give the parent of a 17-year-old killed by a random sniper the same chance at satisfaction as those of a 17-year-old killed for being gay or Jewish or black—or a transvestite.

And there's plenty of guilt to go around in the death of Eddie Araujo. Most parents and schools refuse to teach diversity, and I don't mean these stopgap anti-bullying programs some schools have set up where a few students and teachers try and persuade kids to be tolerant or report name-calling. I mean by incorporating into all school curriculum, in a very matter-of-fact way, different lifestyles, different people, different ideals and ways of thinking. How many schools would employ known transvestites or transsexuals, even if the person was qualified? Parents would scream—the same parents who say they're all for equal rights. NIMBY. Not in My Back Yard. Gay teachers are fine, just not for my kid (well, excluding PE). Transsexuals, transvestites, well, I suppose they're OK, but at some other school.

And what about this veil of politically-correct-Kumbaya-we-are-the-world-let's-join-hands-and-sing notion that we pass on to our minority children? We may want it to be true, but believing it can be hazardous to our children's health. Someone should have told Araujo until they were blue in the face that no matter how hard we want the world to sing in perfect harmony, there are those out there who would kill him for no other reason than the fact that he is different. Someone should have prevented him, physically if need be, from getting into "normal" situations with "normal" students under the pretense that he was "normal" himself, because he was not normal. He was different. He was an outsider, someone outside the normal frame of reference.

I would like to live in a world where we don't kill things we don't understand, but I work in media, and unfortunately, I know that's not this world. All we do is kill things we don't understand, from men who dress like women and hide it to brown people who speak foreign tongues and worship odd gods. And as for schoolchildren—who ever warned Araujo that young males are exponentially more predisposed than any other creature on the planet to commit an act of violence against anything that challenges their own ideas of the world? And that predisposition boils over into frightening likelihood when they find out that someone who may have appealed to them on a sexual level was pulling the wool over their eyes. That's why they bash: They are afraid, they are challenged, they are ignorant, they are the embodiment of a lifetime of puritanical notions mixed up with the most aggressive nature.

I am not a parent, so I can't speak for the Araujo family. I don't know Araujo's home life. But I know if my child was a biological male who dressed like a woman, I would get him out of any rural town as soon as the first dress went on. I would find a big city with a special school program for gay or lesbian youth and at least hedge my child's chances of survival through the teen years. I wouldn't stay in Newark, no matter how progressive it may have seemed. Should my child be safe in Newark? Yup. But that's just not real-world thinking. There are "places for people like us," and we'd better stay in them until we are equipped to venture out into hostile territory. And trust me, it can be hostile being different in the mainstream. Ghettos serve a purpose, even urban ones—as much as they segregate, they also protect. And while I am a firm advocate of integration, 17-year-olds who cross-dress aren't ready to be introduced into senior year at High School USA.

What those boys did was wrong, plain and simple. What Ms. Brown did—egging on the guys, announcing Araujo's sexuality—was equally as wrong in my book and almost a death sentence. Was it a hate crime? Yes, it was a crime born of hate, but again, what capital offense isn't? Should they receive a more severe sentence because it was a hate crime? No, they should receive the maximum sentence because they killed an innocent human being unprovoked, regardless of motive.

Should Araujo have known he was flirting with disaster? Absolutely, and if he knew and did nothing about it, someone around him should have loved him enough to help him see the danger for him in so many situations. His wasn't to be an easy life, and acting like the world has to accept you for who you are is naive. The world doesn't.

In fact, the world isn't very accepting of much these days when it comes to different lifestyles. The puritanical winds are again sweeping through the land, empowering bigots and zealots to verbally or physically disparage that which doesn't conform to what they feel is right and proper. And in an effort to believe that the world can be a better place (which, incidentally, it can be, and is at times) we often forget that we sometimes need to give harsh, real-world advice to those we love, even if that advice is that you don't always fit in and it could be dangerous simply to be you in some situations. That any situation could be a risk, and you must learn to assess those risks before entering a situation—and know very well how to get out of a bad situation safely once you see trouble coming.

Eddie "Gwen" Araujo is dead. He's not coming back, and we live in a world where some would say, "Hey, that's what he gets for living like that." Well, that *is* what he got for living like that. So, how do we reconcile that still-prevalent attitude—death for the different—with our determination that no one like Araujo should die in that way ever again? The answer is elusive, but we'd better find it quickly, and honestly. We'd better face harsh facts and real truths and formulate a plan. These kinds of deaths are happening too often, from Matthew Shepard to Brandon Teena, Billy Jack Gaither to Gwen Araujo. Those who would kill don't seem to be getting any less inclined, and the potential victims don't seem to be getting any smarter. That's a dangerous equation, and the by-product has been one too many funerals.

Lover or Life?

In every relationship there comes a pivotal point, a fork in the road when you have to decide whether the person you're with is simply your lover or your life. It's at that point when you must decide: Is this really the person with whom I will build my future? The only person in the world whom I can imagine living with and can't imagine living without? Is this the *real* thing, or is it something a little less? Is it something wonderful, something grand, and yet something that could in fact be over? Or is it like oxygen?

For a friend of mine, it came when his lover moved out while he was at work. Their relationship hadn't been perfect—in fact, it had been downright rocky at times. But it had been going on for more than eight years. Then one day the lover was gone, moved away—to get his head straight, to start anew, to concentrate on work and paying bills, to become a stronger, more mature person. All noble goals for an "I" but not for the "we." *We* make decisions that are best for *us,* not *you* for *you* and *me* for *me.* Contrary to public belief, a *you* and a *me* in a relationship doesn't make an *us.*

My friend wondered what to do, stating that he wanted to

go on with the relationship, to pick up the pieces, to help his lover with his goals. That's decision time. If his lover is life, then there are no questions, no decisions. In that case my friend should simply find a job in the area where his partner moved, call him, tell him that if he's willing to work at being an *us,* he'd like to follow him and support him in his quest for self-improvement. He should tell him that he'd rather turn his life here upside down than live without him. It may seem unfair, but no one ever said the *f* in life is for "fair," and if your partner is your life, you do what you can to save your life—within reason. Moving is within reason.

But if your partner is just that, a lover; if the bad outweighs the good; if life is nothing more than a series of problems to fix instead of experiences together to be enjoyed—well, lives should be saved; not all lovers have to be.

Maybe it's not someone moving on, but a challenge—regardless, a crucial point of decision will happen in every relationship. There will be a request, a situation, a challenge so great that one or both will have to decide just how much the relationship is worth. For me, it was never a question. As my friends will attest, I would have followed Andrew to Boise, Ida., if he had asked (bitching and moaning all the way). I would have found a way to entertain, to write, be on TV, be in film, on radio, from a mountaintop if I had to, if that's what was needed. But he would have never asked, because as we all know, being an *us* is about compromise. It's about each partner knowing that he is the other's life and that he holds his partner's life as precious as his own. When that kind of reverence is given to a relationship, a lot of changes and decisions can be made where both lives survive, and thus the life of the couple survives as well.

The problem lies in that we think we are supposed to be two independent individuals within a relationship, coexisting as one. That's new age psychobabble. The very nature of coupling, of being together, is symbiotic. It's codependency at its best. And it's sublime. There is nothing like needing someone, wanting someone so much that absence almost causes physical pain. There is nothing wrong with wanting to grow up and grow older with someone, and knowing that you'll be a richer, better person for it, better than if you were on your own. And there's nothing wrong with making compromises or sacrifices, even major life changes, to keep that person, that life, so long as that street goes both ways. There is nothing wrong with putting the self on hold for the success of the *us,* the *we.*

Oh, now I've done it. I've reopened the thinking of 100 years ago, when women were supposed to blindly follow their man no matter what was best for them; when one person in the relationship was expected to give up his or her life and assimilate into the life of the other. Nonsense. However, sometimes one member of the relationship is going to be called upon to give up more than he wants to or feels he should have to. That's where the question enters: Is he my lover or my life?

Ultimately, it's about happiness. In my case, my happiness was with Andrew. The trappings of our happiness were secondary—our house, our careers, our social circles. Yes, those were all pieces of the puzzle that made up our lives, but they weren't the majority of the pie. The majority was time with him—loving, laughing, arguing, simply being alive with him. In Los Angeles or Paris, Big Bear or Barstow. Anyplace truly was home as long as he was there, because he wasn't my lover; he was, in fact, my life.

But as my lover's death has proved, your life can change just as your lover can. Short of the permanence of that, however, it's always a choice. Where your life leads and what it is made up of is a conscious choice. Being realistic helps. Make sure when deciding between lover or life that you have a realistic view of the relationship and of your life in it, of your place. If you reach that fork in the road and can't imagine your life any other way than with your partner, then do what you must to keep the life you want (short of boiling a rabbit). If you step back and realize you're in love more with the idea than the person, move on, for the sake of both of you.

You see, you only have one life, and that includes the relationship that could become your life. If you're wasting time in an empty relationship, one that is less than perfect, then you are depriving yourself of your real life, the life waiting for you when you find the person who makes the question of "lover or life" irrelevant, the person whom you know in your heart, in your soul, in your fiber that you are supposed to be with, the person who becomes your life.

Too High a Price

OK, I've done it. I've had a one-night stand. It took 18 months after the death of my partner, and a few kamikaze shots, but it happened. There I was, at a club. I had just dropped my sister at the airport after Thanksgiving and really, truly needed a drink. There was a cute redhead with a goatee. (Did I mention my late husband was a redhead with a goatee?) I wasn't looking, but he found me. We talked. We laughed. After sobering up over chatting and tea at a local coffeehouse, I drove him home. We stopped by my house. We Jacuzzied. And the rest, as they say, is history.

He was HIV-positive, told me straight away. No big deal for me, since my late husband was as well. It was nice of him to tell me, though.

God, how new to this I am! Are my condoms expired? Where are the "supplies"? Do I even have any more Wet? There I was, in bed with a stranger, after 13½ years. Doing *exactly* what I preach against. He kept saying how cute I was. I kept asking him if he needed more light. He loved it all, or so he said: The nipple rings, the tattoos, all my new body modifications—the pack mentality toward self-mutilation that I've been party to over the past year (seven tattoos and two piercings to date). We kissed. We did it all. And woke up the next morning and did it again—all safely, of course, but all nonetheless.

Then he left. I drove him home and bid goodbye. He said to call him. I said I would, knowing I probably wouldn't.

Why? Well, first and foremost, I'm a chicken and I hate it. You see, I loved Andrew, my late husband, with every ounce of fiber in me. When we first started dating in the late 1980s everyone told me not to because he had HIV. I told them I would never, ever think that way. And yet in 2002, having buried so many friends and Andrew, truth be told, I don't want to be that close to HIV right now. I just don't. Protease inhibitors, T-cell counts, viral loads, research, clinical trials, the Medscape HIV newsletter—I haven't had to study all of that for 18 months, and right now, I just can't. I'm in the middle of a wrongful-death lawsuit, a book, radio, TV...all feeble excuses, I know. Because if there were a spark, I wouldn't care, and I know it. I'd jump right in like I did with Andrew.

And that's just it. No spark. I mean, the sex was good, but it's the ultimate in Chinese fast food. It's filling while you're enjoying it, but an hour later, nothing, empty. My roommate Sean tells me that's how it always is, casual sex. So, I ask: Why do men, particularly gay men, spend so much of their time trying to find it, get it, have it? Why is almost everything from magazine covers to doctors' ads, travel destinations to social engagements, designed around the possibility of getting it? It seems so useless. I know *I'm* opting out. I am.

Who was this person, really? How stupid was I to bring a stranger to my home, my inner sanctum? In my car? Did he have anything other than HIV? Can I trust him? (No.) And for what? I mean, really, is getting off that fantastic? Nope, not with a stranger, I'll tell you that.

Oh, my God, I'm my father! I'm those voices that say sex without connection just isn't worth it. Because I've had the other, the sex with love, for 12 years, and nothing beats it. The rest is a waste of time. How much money would be saved if we could all just see that? The loneliness that drives men to the bedroom isn't going to be filled by the sex act—in fact, I have never felt more alone than today. All casual sex did was make me miss what I had even more.

Maybe in a year I'll feel differently. Maybe it's too soon after the death (18 months). Maybe this wasn't a great first time, the right situation. Who knows? But it just seems to me that someone has sold us a bill of goods that casual sex, and our right to have it, is da bomb. Well, for me, it's da dud. It's like a bowel movement—a natural body function, but nothing to write home about.

And what happens now? He's calling, wanting to see me again. I don't want to. God, I'm evil. If the situation were reversed, I'd be hurt. Look at all the baggage that comes with just one little body-function release. I don't know why I don't want to see him again. He's cute, kind (so far), interesting on the surface. But to me he represents a necessary step, something I had to do, a lesson to learn but nothing more.

I'm compelled to think about another casual-sex experience. At a local gay restaurant-bar that I go to for lunch, a "straight" server had sex with a female server. A one-night sort of thing, much like my own, casual. Now she's pregnant, and they're going to run off to Florida, go to school by day, and let her parents take care of the child while they carve out an existence. Maybe they'll marry; they don't know, since they're not in love. It's such a game, and the child is now a game piece, and all over a casual encounter.

And that's the point. I've realized from my one-night tryst that there is no such thing as casual sex. Not anymore, and maybe there never was. To those who would say, "Oh, it's fun sometimes just to get laid," I would say, "Sure, but at what emotional price? What do we give up for that night? What have we given up for years under the guise that it's natural, we're animals, we're meant to have lots of sex—we're men." Maybe it's the gay man in me saying, *Wait a minute, there is more!* And then another voice says, *Does there have to be each time?* We've been told no. I disagree. That's the easy answer. I would have to say a resounding yes. There must be a connection of sorts, a trust, and an excitement. Animal attraction is great; lust, passion, it's all fine. But if it ends there, it simply isn't good enough. And we've settled for so long. Perhaps it's time to rethink. Perhaps it's time to demand as much from sex as we do from other areas of our life. Perhaps it's not so casual after all.

Will I do it again? Maybe; I don't know. I can't know that 100%. But I know it won't be casual. Today, it's just not worth it. And it's easier to want sex, emotionally, than to have it with strangers. Old-fashioned ideals? Well, maybe some old-fashioned ideals aren't so antiquated after all.

Could this be maturity? I remember the bathhouses, the bars, and the bookstores. It all seemed fine at the time. Now I look back and think, *What were we thinking?* And that's just it; we weren't. The mind is not involved in casual sex, just the other body parts. The problem? The mind can only stay out of it for so long.

I know the next time some cute man wants to jump into bed, he'll have to take me out first. Perhaps a few times. I'll have to know more about him than the fact that he looks good in jeans and wants me. It's not enough anymore. Maybe it never was.

A Kiss Is Still a Kiss

A recent study by German scientists discovered that the way we kiss, whether we turn our heads to the right or left, is probably determined in the womb. It also determined that people turn their heads to the right 2–1 when it comes to kissing. Another survey released that same week attributed happier, healthier lives to those who kiss and kiss often: It lowers blood pressure, induces euphoria…heck, it all but cures the common cold.

I had forgotten the power of a kiss. How can one forget? Well, by not doing it. Almost two years ago I lost my partner of 11-plus years. Kissing him was fireworks, from the first day to our final night together. I'll never forget that one. We drove home after a club. We parked in the garage. He was in an obstinate mood. Before we got out of the car, he reached over, grabbed me, and planted a big one on me, tongue and all. Then he released me and said with a laugh "So there" as I sat dazed. That kind of abrupt passion wasn't in his character. It was a welcome shock, and now, one that I'll remember forever. The next time I kissed him was on his forehead, so very cold, as I said my final goodbye.

Then, tonight, I was out with some friends. One was a special friend, one who is in that gray area between friend and something else...the one you kiss good night quickly but always wonder what it would be like to just go for it. I don't really think about it much, the going for it, with anyone. It's not on the front burner for me.

However, tonight, for some reason, as we got in the car, my friend jokingly started to make out with me. There were a few kisses, deep ones. My heart nearly stopped. Literally, I felt it beat in my chest. It was so clumsy at first. I mean, I truly acted like someone who had never kissed a guy in the front seat of a car before. When we stopped, as quickly as we started and all in good fun, I was dazed. I actually found words hard to form. I laughed it off, but something inside changed.

For in the moments after, I tasted him. It's so funny what you forget. I tasted him and it was wonderful. I haven't "tasted" anyone in some time, and make no mistake, every person has a distinctive taste. Maybe that's why kisses are savored.

But in today's society, we take these gifts, these kisses, for granted. We often pass them out like candy. I've seen so many strangers meet in a club, and before you know it they're examining each other's dental work with their tongues. If only they knew the power of what they're doing, the importance, the sheer beauty. It's intimate, it's wonderful, it's a treasure, a simple kiss. It's not something to be taken lightly, at least not by me, and not anymore.

And what's more, I realize now that I miss it. I understand why people do it so indiscriminantly. It is fun, it's comforting, arousing, it's so very human. Taking it for granted is almost criminal, and sharing it like a breath mint is ludicrous.

You see, the fact is, you have to do it with someone you have feelings for or it's, well, just a kiss. You see, I am connected in some way to this person that I kissed, and that connection is what the kiss embodied. That connection is what every kiss should embody. It's your first touch, your first invasion of their soul, the first part of an intimate journey that could begin and end with the kiss, but a journey nonetheless. It's not just a simple social act, it's so much more. Go without one for a while and you'll be reminded of that.

And a kiss can stir emotions. Mine did. It has left me wanting more, and yet feeling lonelier than ever. I miss my partner, his taste. I can remember it now. That kissing in my front seat tonight brought back the taste of the kissing that took place the fateful night almost two years ago. And it also made me realize that while I grieve, I must also live. And kissing is part of living. I must not shut myself off to such contact and say it doesn't matter, that I can live without it, that I'm not interested. Because I am interested. We all are. We all want to connect to someone, anyone, in that fashion. It's what keeps the online dating services, chat rooms, bars, and social groups going. It's what fuels Valentine's Day and every romantic novel.

Each night, before bedtime, I used to kiss my partner good night. Even if he was asleep, I'd wake him up briefly to kiss good night. Sometimes he'd get annoyed, but after years he not only got used to it but looked forward to it. Should I ever forget, he'd wake me. I never thought I could miss anything so much until tonight. And I know in my heart I'll find it again. Not the same kiss, a different one, but a kiss nonetheless.

I look forward to rejoining the world of the kissing masses one day. But I'll do so with a newfound appreciation of exactly what that kiss is. Tonight, as I still taste the kisses from just a few hours past, I rejoice in my humanity. I celebrate the fact that in these uncertain times some things are still so simple. I feel hope that even through grief, new sensations can emerge, and I revel in the fact that a kiss isn't just a kiss—each one is a new beginning: a new step; a sharing, no matter how minor, of two hearts. It is affection at its purest, and sometimes we need reminders of just how precious affection, human affection, can be.

And by the way, for the German scientists, we both turned to the right.

Searching for a Legacy

New Year's Eve, 2002. While most were toasting with champagne and ringing in 2003, I was pressing a morphine pump and watching Dick Clark in post-op daze. On December 29 I was admitted to the hospital with severe stomach pain, and after much inconclusive testing was taken to surgery on New Year's Eve for an exploratory lapriscopic procedure. The surgeon found a ruptured appendix and perontinitis (infection of the abdomen), cut it out, cleaned it up, and sent me back upstairs in time to miss the New Year.

The next day things got worse instead of better, as the infection--and the drugs used to fight it--were making me even sicker. Soon I was catheterized, wearing a diaper, and stripped of any dignity I may have had entering the hospital. God bless nurses...I would have quit my job if I were my own patient—what a mess. And yet it's funny: I kept hoping for a female nurse. *Please, not a gay male nurse—I just don't want to be seen this way by a stranger, a gay stranger.* Male vanity through and through.

As I sat, plugged in, bags dripping medications into me, not able to get up, I couldn't help but think, *What if this were it? What if this infection gets the better of me? Are my affairs in order?*

You see, up until Andrew's death, everything was in order. We both had wills, powers of attorneys, advance directives, the whole nine yards. But after his death, I'd been slow to change the paperwork, the beneficiaries. I know, statistically, 50% of you reading this don't even have a simple will or any paperwork. Where would my things, my life, end up? You see, I've learned that once you're gone, all you are is stuff and paperwork for the living, details to be handled, assets to be dispersed. And then there's the legacy, what survives you, who you were, who you touched, your family.

I have boxes of Andrew's clothes, waiting for something to be done with them. I can't donate them or sell them—he didn't want that. How many garage sales we saw in San Francisco in the late '80s and early '90s, people getting rid of a dead lover's things. He didn't want that. So I wait, and know I'll find someone to give them to.

Andrew lives on in me, in his niece Heather and nephew Jake, and in his sister. He lives on in his work, his scripts and screenplays, in the children's books that he authored. He lives on in opinion, having shaped mine and the way I use them in my writing and my radio shows. His garden here is tended and cared for with love; expanded, cherished. Our home is maintained, and cherished items, works of art or thrift store finds, are kept and displayed still. It's like the days of old, the palaces, the chateaus, the homes where there was a history, a family, where people lived and died and went on through others. Walk through Buckingham Palace in London—the queen has no problem with family history; it's all on the walls. How many of us have family history on our walls? Paintings of us, our loved ones? Photos? Lineage?

Would there be any of that of me? Would the house be sold off, the garden destroyed? The artwork sold off? Who would cherish the paintings, the land, the legacy? Who would further my work, my views, my life? Who would remember?

Straight people have some sense of permanence. For most, it's through their children. They feel their line will continue, their name, their very DNA, long after they are gone. For most, it is how they make a difference. Some gays and lesbians adopt or have children, but not most. So where is our legacy?

While sitting in the hospital, in the diaper, with a tube up my dick and more in my arm, I had a lot of time to think. And one of the things I realized is that most gay men live for the moment. They structure their lives and relationships like it is all temporary. They live like getting old isn't an option...do what you want when young. Have sex with whom you want whenever you want. Drink if you want. Do drugs if you want. Live well, eat at fine restaurants now, travel now, do everything you want, now.

Maybe it was AIDS that made us feel like we were limited, maybe not. But that attitude sure does explain a lot of our behavior. We live like there's no repercussions, like aging won't really happen. And most don't worry about legacies, about what we leave behind and how. About who we leave behind. Many gay men enter relationships, stay in them for a few months or years, move on. Long term coupling still isn't the norm, and it certainly isn't fostered in our community. And only the most stable have children or adopt. We often don't dump the time and effort needed to foster relationships that last with friends, family, or loved ones. We are quick to write people off: "Oh, I'm over her;" "I'm through with him." When we die, we simply disappear. We need quilt patches to commemorate our lives; otherwise, we'd all but vanish.

At the hospital, I was never alone. My roommate Sean was a saint, always there before work, at lunch, after work. My other friends gathered and rallied, making sure I was all right. When I got out, Andrew's family, my family, came, the kids to cheer me. And I realized, there is my legacy, there it is. These friends, my niece, my nephew, they are how I will go on. My dear friend Karen's children, in their 30s whom I met in their teens...calling me daily. There it all is. They love this house, these things, as much as I do. Heather has used my relationship with Andrew's as the basis for a college paper about same-sex marriage. Jake has done sensitivity training at his high school about gays, citing me and Andrew as positive role models for him in his life. Friends continue to help me with my writing, with my radio show, with my film projects. Publishing them, helping me create them, inspiring me to write them, sharing my work with their friends, bringing it into other's lives.

I am here. And I will go on in small ways when I am gone. But that took work. It took time. It took being a friend, being a family member. It took participating in life and the real world, laying the groundwork, building the foundation. It took not walking away from people, friends, or family, from remembering that all we are is those whom we love. It took making time. It took building a career, staying focused. Overcoming the no's.

I now live, since my 40th birthday, like there's something more. I have stopped drinking completely, two months and counting. I have stopped smoking pot. I am exercising more, losing weight, not for me as much as for them—those who love me. I want to be here for them, watch them all grow and change. And when I go I want to leave them something. I want to build something they will be proud of, and leave it for someone to carry on.

We have a choice: to be temporary, or permanent. We can live like there is no tomorrow, and there will be none. Or we can live like we are in fact part of some eternal fabric, that our lives matter and we make a difference in some way to one, or to many. We can prepare by doing what we need to do while here (meaning the paperwork), and by living in a manner that fosters a sense of permanence. Once we realize we are not bright flames that are here for a moment and then burn out forever, that we are part of it all and have a legacy, our lives and culture will change. We will have a sense of worth.

Gays and lesbians are often seen on the outside of things, the outside of family units, the outside of social confines. I am saying, Get on the inside. Build an infrastructure on which to fall, because you will fall one day. Dedicate your lives to your friends, your families—ultimately, it will be for yourself. Live like you want to be remembered—if you want to be remembered as loving, caring, a friend and strong family member, then live that way. Take responsibility for your life, because it will become someone else's responsibility. What you do in the bar, bedroom, office, or living room eventually not only affects you but those around you who love and care for you. You have a responsibility to yourself, to them, and to your legacy. Live like you have one and you will. Live like all is temporary, with no roots, no grounding forces, no focus, and you'll end up a name on a piece of paper someplace, a plaque in a field looked at by many but remembered by few.

You're a Fag—So What?

"You there, gay boy, you're a fag. That's right, you, you're a queer. You're gay. In fact, I know someone who's slept with you. You know what? It was me, I slept with you! That's right, you're gay! And I'm going to tell the world..."

Of course, if I do tell anyone, or even just say it out loud, you can sue me and demand $10 million. At least that's what Tom Cruise did when someone said it about him. In fact, many people have gotten settlements for being called gay, regardless of whether they were or not. It appears having the gay moniker attached to you is slanderous, libelous—it's downright litigious.

Even Liberace sued. Can you imagine?

For $10 million, you can call me anything, even a Christian conservative Republican. Well, maybe $20 million.

Why is the allegation of gayness so litigious? Because it's not nice to call someone a criminal if they're not. You see, part of these settlements stem from the fact that in many states same-sex sodomy is still illegal, a punishable crime. So if you allege someone is gay, you are also alleging that they are a criminal, by implying they engage in criminal activity. You've slandered them.

Now, there's not a soul reading this who buys just that. We're all a little smarter. Truth be told, being labeled gay for a star (or anyone, for that matter) is not about sodomy laws; it's about the fact that being a known homosexual is seen as harmful to career and social life. It's like being branded an outcast, and who wants that?

I say poppycock.

If we are ever to achieve equality and fairness, then the courts and public alike need to take away the power of such words, at least from a legal standpoint. Is being gay so bad, the very idea of it, that it's worth money in court? Only if it is, in fact, a horrible thing, a disease, a scourge that must be quelled. But truth be told, being gay isn't so bad at all, and being called gay isn't the worst thing that could happen to a person. It's not even high on the list, or shouldn't be, and it's time courts removed it from the realm of things that are actionable.

For instance, Cruise shouldn't have gotten a settlement from the person who alleged he was gay or alleged a sexual encounter. If Cruise did not get hired for a film, didn't get a job, was discriminated against in some way because of the allegations, then he should prove it: sue his prospective employers for discrimination on the basis of perceived sexual orientation (which doesn't require that a person actually *be* gay) and get financial damages from those parties. Specific parties. But there's no one to sue there, because these allegations have been around since he started acting and haven't hurt his career a bit. In fact, they may have helped. So he has no one to sue. He has suffered no damages other than being called a queer. And quite frankly, that's just not good enough anymore.

Yes, it can be damaging. My roommate recently had the word FAG etched into his locker at work. He was devastated. A week later they did it again. Suddenly, all the baggage of being an outcast in a small town in Ohio, the pain of being a gay youth in a cloistered environment, it all came back—from one little word. A police report was filed; it was classified as a hate crime. But, as much as I love him, I have to say, Why not just paint your locker pink and put a heart around the word? After all, he *is* a big ol' fag. It's a statement of fact presented in a brutal fashion that's meant to hurt, but it only hurts if we, and the courts, continue to allow it to. Perhaps at minimum he should have scratched in the word "Duh..."

The problem is that baggage. We won't let go of the fact that, like the word *nigger,* the words *fag, queer, gay* are rooted in years of hatred and oppression, and we feel that oppression every time someone says, writes, or otherwise conveys the words. It's not the words that hurt us, or the fact of being labeled a gay person. It's the reminder that there are people out there with so much anger and hatred at something they don't understand that they're willing to lash out at us just because we're different. That's what hurts.

So the only way we won't feel that hurt anymore is to disempower the words.

You don't know how much flack I get on my radio show when I say I'm a queer, or when Andrew would call me a big old fag. Gays just don't like that language, and they call or e-mail to tell me that all the time. Well, I call other gays "queer," "fag," "dyke," etc. I have reclaimed those words for my usage, and I don't use them maliciously.

Once, while at a personal appearance, I was walking to the stage, and a young surfer type as I walked by yelled "Fag!" I stopped and said, "Honey, is that a news flash for you? Did it take all of your 20 brain cells to figure that out, because if it did, I'm doing something wrong. Of course I'm a queer. You think a straight man could have such flair?" He shut up. And was laughed at. And it was over. No courts, no lawyers, no violence. I took away his power.

Being called gay is not a slam. It is not a crime and should not be actionable. As sodomy laws change, so will these cases, and then what will all those poor souls out there do, those who think being called a queer or gay is the end of their professional life or a personal trip to hell? They'll just have to get over it, and so will we. Get over it. You are a fag, a queer, a dyke, a big homo. You're Gay. And if you're not, your life isn't ruined because somebody thinks you are. Only you have the power to ruin your life; adjust your attitude and any outside power is gone.

And before all you politically correct types start firing off rebuttals, remember this: It's all about intent. Killing someone and scrawling the word FAG on their forehead is not the same as alleging that celebrity, that boss, or that neighbor is gay. Even so, we do need to get to a point where we no longer allow the words themselves, or the mere allegation of homosexuality, to be deemed as damaging, unless our cultural self-esteem is genuinely that low. Unless we truly believe that we are wrong, that being gay is bad and that being called gay can in fact ruin a life. It's made mine far more interesting. Yup, I'm a *big* ol' fag, and damned proud of it. If you write it on my door, it's vandalism, nothing more. If you call me it in print, it's an observation, not a slam.

I have realized that the only way evil wins is for good people to do nothing when faced with it. It's time we remove this particular "evil" from the courts, from our ranks, and society as a whole. There was a time you could actually win a libel case because someone alleged you were black or had black blood in you. Now we laugh at such things. Isn't it time we start laughing at cases like Tom Cruise's as well?

Red, White, and Blue: Still Part of the Rainbow

It's a time of war. It's a time of patriotism. God knows I've tried. In 2001, when King George asked us all to fly flags in honor of September 11, I erected a 22-foot flagpole in front of my house and proudly flew a large American flag because I am in fact an American—whether America likes it or not. Of course, two weeks ago someone stole my flag. Yup, lowered it and took it. There's a good American for you. So I replaced it, but I almost wondered why.

I was on the radio a few weeks ago, and a listener scolded me, saying how dare I criticize the Bush administration's plans in Iraq since I have never served in the military. Obviously, I don't know what it means to be an American, and I have no voice since I have not been in the military. What an asinine attitude. Not many Americans go in the military any longer, at least college-educated ones, or children of middle-class or upper-income Americans. Hell, only a handful of senators and congressmen have children in the military.

Of course, my retort to him was that the military doesn't want me. They won't let me serve openly as who and what I am, and I, quite frankly, think closets are for clothes. But then I began to think about it and realized, hell, the United States doesn't want me. Let me rephrase that: It wants my tax dollars to support schools for children I'll never have. It wants my money to support a military in which I cannot openly serve. It wants my money to run a state and country in which I legally cannot marry simply because of the sex of whom I love. It wants my tax dollars to support a criminal justice system that in numerous states will prosecute me for the kind of sex I have, while leaving my heterosexual counterparts alone for the same thing. It wants my money to pay for a war in the Middle East to be fought over oil when I believe we should not be there. Yup, about the only thing America wants from me, or any other gay and lesbian, is our money. The rest we have to fight for or shut up and take. Because we're good Americans it's still the best game in town, and we can love it or leave it.

I have often said our civil rights movement will come when gays and lesbians organize a national tax revolt. When every gay or lesbian person simply refuses to pay taxes until the government equals the playing field. And work stoppages. The same techniques Gandhi used. Sure, folks would be prosecuted, serve jail time, all of that. But think about what the U.S. government would do if 10% of the taxpayers, many of whom are in the higher tax brackets, suddenly refused to pay. Hit them where it hurts, in the wallet, and policies would change. But alas, it's just a pipe dream.

So what is it to be a good, patriotic gay person these days? Given that we are not all going to pack up and move to Amsterdam, what does it mean to be a good American in a country that doesn't want us?

Well, first it means not admitting defeat. That's why I fly my flag: open defiance. You see, I realize all that's wrong here but still proudly say, "Yes, I'm here, I'm American, and I believe in many of the ideals the forefathers laid out for us." I know that in time, a few hundred years, historians will look back at this overly religious, prejudicious time in American history and remark how primitive and exclusionary it was.

And I vote. A novel idea, but given how few Americans do it these days, one of the best ideas around—particularly for gays and lesbians. And I don't vote my sexuality—that is, support a candidate for his or her views on gay rights alone. I vote my conscience and what I believe to be best not only for me but for the country as a whole. For instance, I'm a tried-and-true Democrat, but after interviewing Sen. John McCain at length and reading his policies, I would have been hard-pressed to choose between him and Al Gore.

I also forgive. I know that most of what is happening today in American politics, most of the problems for gays and lesbians, are rooted in the mingling of religion and the White House. Separation of church and state is myth, and most of our laws and policies are strongly rooted in religion. Hell, we're about to launch a full-fledged Crusade—the Christians against the Muslims. King George even uttered the word "crusade," albeit by "accident." The oppression we feel is from thousands of years of mindless followers of a philosophy based in myth and not fact. The problem is that somewhere along the line we interpreted God's law as man's law. When we can get God out of the White House, the statehouses, and the courthouses, because America will have realized that morality is not tied to religion but to a fundamental understanding of what is right—that is, fair—and what is wrong, things will be a lot better for gays and lesbians, and the country.

So as a patriotic gay American I forgive the mindless zealots who base their policies on a book that could easily be a work of fiction just as much as it could be fact, and who use it as a shield for the real prejudice and bigotry they have fostered in their own hearts. I forgive their fear of anything different.

I once wrote an article titled "American First, Hyphenate Second" about how the 9/11 tragedy took away the monikers *gay American, black American,* and *Muslim-American*; it simply made us all Americans. That spirit lasted a while after the attacks, and now we've gone back to the divisive lot we were before. Didn't take long for the political parties to redraw their lines and stop working together, or for members of diverse communities to forget the bond that binds us all, and instead go back to our ghettos and our ranks. As a patriotic gay American I will continue to try and cross those boundaries through action and attitude, by seeing myself not as part of a minority but as part of the majority—the majority of people who see themselves as Americans first. They're out there.

And as a patriotic gay American I continue to pay taxes to the system that refuses to recognize me unless compelled by force, and I will demand more from it. I participate. Perhaps that's the only real patriotism we as gays and lesbians have available to us: the ability to participate even though many would have us not. The country was founded by outcasts, and we as such, are now fighting another revolution inside our own borders. As revolutionaries, we must continue to fight within the boundaries of the law, using the very system that would oppress us to gain freedom, remembering that the freedoms afforded in that document we all cling to, the Constitution, indeed still—especially—apply to us.

What does it mean to be gay and patriotic? It means to accept this land and its residents for their good and bad, and still be able to lift a flag in front of your house with stars and stripes and not just a rainbow. It means to look a military person in the eye and say to them, "I appreciate your service, and one day, when your establishment stops its exclusionary practices, I would be happy to serve next to you. In the meanwhile, I'll continue to pay your salary." It means speaking out through dollars and deeds to create a better land, and silencing, in the same way, those who are oppressive. It means not only forgiving the huddled masses who mindlessly ascribe to whatever they are being sold by slick politicians, but presenting those masses with a new product through example, or by legal force if necessary. It means knowing how the system works so you can not only be a part of it but use it to your advantage and your community's. And it means remembering that without red, white, and blue, there would be no rainbow.

Ten Hours

Ten hours. In 10 hours I'll be sitting in a superior court in Long Beach, Calif., and waiting as a judge hears oral arguments in what my lawyer says is a case of "First Impression"—meaning, it's the first case of its kind in the state.

Six hundred forty days ago my lover died right in front of me. Two hours of agony and it was over, for him at least. For me it goes on, every day. What happened was wrong, every medical expert I talk to agrees. But that is so lost right now. All that matters, all that's mattered for 20 months, is whether I was legally his spouse, his partner, his heir.

Today I went and read all the briefs, the legal papers filed on my behalf and on the behalf of the hospital. They were filled with words like *alleged domestic partner* and *since Mr. Bouley was not an immediate family member*. I read and read and read, hundreds of pages. Not one of them said anything about how my partner Andrew died. Not one time did lawyers for the defendants—the hospital— try to vindicate their client or justify what happened that night.

It all has to do with me. I have no right to sue, they argue.

I had no relationship to my lover of nearly 12 years. No relationship at all.

Tomorrow a judge I've never met, a woman I do not know, will sit and decide whether I was Andrew's spouse, if the 11-plus years we had together legally mattered. If the nights of comforting him during night sweats, the times in the ER telling him he was going to be all right, the trips to Stanford University to get him on a drug study, the slow dancing in the living room almost every day, the smile on both our faces our first day on the job at KFI as we became the first gay male couple to ever do such a job, the fights over God knows what, the jealousy he put up with on my part, the final kiss on his cold forehead, the sleepless nights I've endured since his death, his final scream that rings in my ear daily, the acceptance into his family, the laughter I still share with his niece and nephew, the hugs I give his sister, the good night kisses we gave each other every night of our relationship—all that and so much more—this woman will rule if all that made me his spouse.

Andrew died May 21, 2001. At the time there was no legislation in California to allow me to sue as his domestic partner. Only spouses and biological relatives in the state had the legal right to sue someone responsible for the wrongful death of a loved one. Domestic partners—whether of 30 days or 30 years—need not apply. Soon after Andrew's death a woman named Sharon Smith filed suit against the people she believed were responsible for the horrible dog-mauling death of her partner, Diana Alexis Whipple, in the hallway of their apartment building. She too was told by the lawyers for the defense that she had no standing to sue. A judge thought differently: Since the state doesn't allow gay and lesbian couples to become legal "spouses," the judge decided, it was an unreasonable requirement that Sharon and Alexis be married before Sharon could sue for Alexis's wrongful death. The two women were, for all intents and purposes, spouses. Sharon's case was allowed to proceed; she settled out of court.

Thanks in part to Sharon Smith's tenacity and her testimony before the state legislature, on January 1, 2002, a new law went into effect in California. AB 25 changed California Civil Code of Procedure section 377.60 to allow domestic partners to sue in wrongful-death cases. I filed my lawsuit that same January, within the one-year statute of limitations since Andrew's death.

Dates, timing, mishaps—that's all it's been since that final, awful trip to the ER. Andrew died too early for AB 25 to apply, they'll argue tomorrow. Our domestic-partnership agreement was filed too late, they'll say. It was signed and notarized on December 5, 2000, and mailed immediately thereafter. But it was not processed by the state until after his death. No one knows why. The Secretary of State's office doesn't save envelopes, so there's no proof that we mailed it when I say we did. Mishap after mishap.

And here I sit, feeling so alone in the middle of it all. So empty. Andrew is gone and I may never get to bring to justice those people who everyone I talk to agrees are responsible— or, really, *irresponsible*—in his death, because I'm a man and he was a man, and the fact that we loved each other is not legally relevant. Or so they will argue. His parents may sue, and they say they support my right to sue, and that's something. But it's just not enough.

Tomorrow is a first. Sacramento is keeping an eye on it. Does Section d of 377.60—which says "This applies to all causes of actions on or after January 1, 1993" mean we're covered? Well, that's up to judicial interpretation. Was it the intent of the legislature to grandfather in those cases in which "cause" occurred after January 1, 1993, but before the law took effect? Up to a judge. Does it matter that I met the statue of limitations and that AB 25 passed within that year after Andrew's death? Or did my cause of action die with Andrew?

Up to a judge. Does the term *spouse* as referenced in 377.60 apply to gays and lesbians in committed relationships, as was argued successfully in the Sharon Smith case? Up to a judge.

All I know is, tomorrow I'll walk in, sit down, and in a matter of moments it will be over, and yet only just begun. If it goes badly, we appeal. Which means we'll spend more weeks, months, even years arguing the validity of our relationship. Because we were two men. Someday we might get to actually arguing about what happened that night. But not now, not yet, not tomorrow.

It's like now they're trying to kill us—the us we were for almost 12 years—after they already killed Andrew.

What a sad state of affairs. For all you gay rights activists, thanks, you've come so far. In fact, you've come *just* so far. As you applaud yourself on AB 25, and rightfully so perhaps, I can't help but wonder what a feeble attempt it seems to be to fix such a broken system. How many gays and lesbians are like me, disempowered in the loss of their spouses because the law said we were nothing to one another, just friends, almost strangers, before the passage of AB 25? How and why have we tolerated such second-class citizenship for so long?

I will fight. Win or lose tomorrow, I will fight. I have no choice. Maybe if I win, others will be able to fight and win as well. But just for once, I wish I wasn't the first. It's been a lifetime of firsts for me: first gay person to do this or that, first to achieve this or that professional goal, blah, blah, blah. Big deal. Really. I mean it. Big deal. Because tomorrow, to the court, I'm just another fag who loved some other fag who died and all the years together mean nothing in the courtroom to a bunch of people who could care less about the real morality of the case. Tomorrow, if I lose, I won't be the first. Or the second, or the 10,001st.

Here are some firsts I'd like to see: Any seated judge who has thrown out a case out like this because it was two men or two women should be removed from the bench. Any lawyer should be disbarred if their client's case was dismissed because that client's partner had no standing under the law due to not being able to legally get married.

Here is what I want to say to these people: What you are doing, and have done, is hurt countless hundreds or thousands of people. And for what? To protect some antiquated law? To save some rich client? Do you think gays and lesbians who have lost partners are money-grubbing perverts out to destroy the rule of law and bring down innocent clients? No, we are grieving *spouses* trying to right a wrong, no matter what you in the courts and the law firms and the legislature had to say about it up until January 1, 2002, and no matter what they may have to say tomorrow. You told us for years that only spouses could sue, but you didn't let us marry. Every lawmaker, judge, and malpractice/wrongful-death lawyer should be ashamed for letting this go on for so very long.

So tomorrow the gavel will fall and my next step will be clear. But as I sit here tonight I just want to hold what I have left of Andrew close in my heart and apologize to him. Andrew, I am so sorry that I can't fight harder, that the courts are trying to block me even from letting us have our day in court to really talk about what happened to you that terrible night. I'm sorry that the 11-plus years you spent with me amounts to nothing under the law and that I can't do more for you. I'm sorry that I couldn't save you that night—I tried so hard. I yelled, I cried, I pleaded, and I failed. And as hard as I try tomorrow, I may not be able to bring you justice in court for what happened to you that night. Bringing the light of justice to that night may be left up to your mom and dad, and I don't know that you'd want them to go through this. I'm sorry it may be left up to them. I'm sorry we never mailed our DP agreement years earlier instead of waiting for our 10th anniversary. Maybe it would have helped, maybe the state or post office wouldn't have messed up. I'm sorry you died before AB 25 passed, if you had to die at all. I'm sorry I don't want to face the media tomorrow, when you know I used to live to be in front of a microphone or camera. I'm sorry I feel selfish and just want to scream at the injustice of all of this. Because, after all, I'm still here to fight. And that's why I will, my dearest Andrew. I'll fight, not because it's easy, not because I want to, not because I'll win, but because I can. It's the only way you can still have any justice, so I must.

To any gay or lesbian person out there who lost a partner to wrongful death and couldn't have your day in court, I apologize for the hideous injustice of the United States. To those of you who live in states where bills like AB 25 don't exist, you'd better start rallying some officials.

I will die knowing Andrew Howard was my spouse. I don't need 377.60 to define it for me. They can make me doubt my sanity, but not my relationship. He was my husband. I fought with him, and now I'll fight for him. I'm left with no choice. I'll keep going to court. And maybe, just maybe one day, states won't make those who have suffered such a loss relive the tragedy again and again through their institutionalized bigotry.

Our Civic Duty

There it was, in my mailbox, the dreaded jury summons, and this time there was no getting out of it. I have in the past, but now they've made it very hard to avoid. So one day during my assigned week my jury group was called to appear, and the next day down I went.

I entered the jury assembly room and soon had to watch a video. It spoke of the honor of being a juror, of my civic duty to my city, my country, and my fellow man. It spoke of how being a juror relates right back to the fundamentals of the Constitution. It was so patriotic I wanted to wrap myself in an American flag and sing something.

It was ironic, as I sat on the sixth floor of the Long Beach Superior Courthouse in the jury orientation room—ironic that just one week previous I was on the third floor of the same building, in front of Superior Court Judge Margaret Hay. I was in front of this judge fighting for the right to sue Long Beach Memorial Hospital and Dr. Stephen Kooshian for wrongful death in the loss of my partner, Andrew Howard. As the jurors' instructional tape spoke of my duty to America, I wondered, What is America's duty to me? I had to fight for the basic right to seek justice for the loss of my partner, a right granted without question or hesitation to mixed-sex couples, a right denied to me because I was a man who loved a man.

It amazed me, the entire process. During the hearing to determine if my partner of nearly 12 years and I had actually been more than mere acquaintances, the opposing counsel got to say whatever they wanted, true or false. Lawyers for Dr. Kooshian—a doctor who advertises here in Long Beach in the gay paper, the *Blade,* that he's the one for the gay community—his lawyer argued that Andrew and I were nothing and that I had no legal standing to sue because of his unjust death, that our 11-plus years together did not make us a couple under the law when he died. How amusing was that. A doctor who says he prides himself on serving the gay community turns his back on a valid relationship out of his own self-interest. His lawyers weren't arguing that he had done nothing wrong in managing Andrew's care. The question of how and why Andrew died didn't come up. The lawyers were simply avoiding the subject by saying that under the law I was nothing to Andrew and therefore couldn't even ask the questions. Good lawyering. That's what it's all about.

So here it was, a week later, and I was sitting in the jury room. Soon I was called to be on a panel. I made it; I was juror number six. It was a case of domestic abuse. The trial lasted a few days, and it was a farce. It was the same thing I went through in my case, all about good lawyering—not about the truth, facts, justice, but about who could put on the best show. Proof that the jury system doesn't work as it is and needs reform, but that's another column.

Despite the lawyer show, we discussed the facts of the case in the jury room and we found the defendant guilty. When I was done, I was thanked for my service, for doing my duty.

Duty. Yes, I have a duty to America. But America's been a little lax on fulfilling its duties to me. I'm supposed to have the right to life, liberty, and the pursuit of happiness. But I guess that comes with certain limitations. The life promised appears to be the life the current mood of the country or the White House administration deems appropriate; the liberties promised are those that are granted under laws based in Christian beliefs that oppose my very existence; and the happiness extends only to feeling joy about things within the confines of what society sets up as normal. Step outside any of that and suddenly it's quite all right to deny a person those all-American rights. If your life and happiness is with someone of the same sex, then forget about liberties or justice. If you want those, you're going to have to fight. And you may not always win. So far, I haven't.

Judge Hay granted the demurrer, as the jargon goes, and in her ruling said that I had no standing to file a lawsuit. AB 25 hadn't passed yet when Andrew died and at that time I couldn't legally marry Andrew, so I wasn't legally his spouse, as the law requires. End of story. Everyone go home.

Of course, I'll appeal, which is what I knew would happen all along, but what a tremendous waste of time and resources—and without even a peep about the real issue, which is whether Andrew had to die that night in the ER.

That's what I thought about the trial for which I was juror number six: What a tremendous waste of time and resources. And that's what historians will think when they look back on this period in America and in its treatment toward gays and lesbians: What a tremendous waste of time and resources, spent not in the name of justice but in the cause of denying justice, of reconfirming inequality.

I suppose I should have walked away from both experiences with a positive feeling about the court system. After serving on a jury, I should feel at ease that the system does in fact work. After all, the domestic abuser accused in our case went to jail, or at least we convicted him of Corporal Injury of a Cohabitant, and I assume that has jail time associated with it. And after fighting in front of Judge Hay and knowing

I can appeal her ruling, I should feel that at least there's hope, a chance for a redress of grievances, a chance for justice. And yet all I feel is that the system is so busy maintaining the system, it has no idea what it was originally set up for.

And as for civic duty, it remains hard to feel obliged to a community, a state, a country that doesn't really want me as a part of it. The U.S. doesn't want me. Let me rephrase: They want my tax dollars, my money, to support their schools for children I'll never have. They want my money to support a military in which I cannot openly serve. They want my money to run a state and country in which I legally cannot marry simply because of my gender and whom I love. They want my money to support a criminal justice system that in almost every state will refuse to recognize my relationship; that, up until a ruling in 2003 by the Supreme Court, would have prosecuted me under many a state's law for the kind of sex I have while leaving my heterosexual counterparts alone for the same thing. They want my money to pay for a war in the Middle East to be fought over oil when I believe we should not be there. Yup, about the only thing America wants from me, or any other gay and lesbian, is our money. The rest we have to fight for or shut up and pretend to be happy not to have it. We're expected to sit quietly in the back of society's bus because we're good Americans, it's still the best game in town, and we love it or leave it.

Well, I do love it, and I'm not leaving it. I'm here, I'm queer, I'm used to it. I'll fight, and I'll win. And if I don't I'll write about it, I'll talk about it, I'll tell other people about the country that they live in—that's still one liberty I have. In fact, that's the one civic duty we all have. We must share our experiences, our lives, our struggles, our joys, our pains. We must bring our lives to the forefront through whatever means we can, to friends, loved ones, at work, through work. It's our civic duty to demand unrest, to not be complacent. It's our civic duty to remind the community as a whole that we are still a vital, integral part of America. Yes, by serving on juries. Yes, by filing lawsuits when we're wronged, by speaking up and speaking out.

As lawyers wrap themselves in the Constitution and law, as leaders clamor to assure us they are protecting our rights, we must exercise those rights. *Exercise* is the key word here. Think about it. No one really likes exercise; if we did, we wouldn't be a country of obese people. Exercise isn't easy; it's time-consuming and takes up energy. But we must exercise all of our rights, our civic duties, the things that still make us good Americans. And we must do it often.

It is our civic duty to have a voice, one we must exercise daily or lose forever.

Wouldn't Change
a Thing

Below is a letter from the mailbag, written by a 16-year-old listener currently living as a foreign exchange student in Germany. I've left it just the way I received it:

Subject: Changing Homosexuality

Karel:

Okay the subject of my e-mail is a little interesting huh? Well I have been researching these "cure homosexuality" therapists. And what they are saying is VERY convincing (kind of like how we homosexuals try to convince THEM that we're totally NORMAL!) I'm comfortable to be who I am. Gay. But see I'm 16. And I have many friends who are straight. I'm so jealous. Why can't I have that "normal" heterosexual life? I don't want to loose friends because of my sexuality. And you know what, you probably think that if I loose them, then they weren't really my friends. Well you know what...I love my friends. And do I really need my sexuality to potentially make my life difficult in so many aspects?

My friend in USA asked me yesterday that if I could have the choice to wake up tomorrow gay or straight what would I choose. I scared myself. I would really choose straight. I think that I really shocked myself. I had been looking at this therapy and wondering does it really work? CAN homosexuality really be CHANGED!?!?! Can one's orientation be reversed? I'm intrigued. I'm boarder line here. I really am. It's scary. Throw me a bone here... I have heard a lot of horror stories about "treatments" but do you know of anyone this actually worked for? And you know...it's just. I don't know if I would or would not do it. It would make things a lot easier. Much of my depression and thinking revolves around homosexuality. I told myself for the past two years that it's normal! It's okay! I know it is. But...God I can't even put my thoughts into perspective...can you help, you're good at this kind of thing.

Signed,
Your Listener in Germany

To My German Friend:

First, by all accounts from the psychological community, *no,* homosexuality cannot be "changed." It is not a psychological disorder. Research into "reparative" therapies is somewhat skewed, since it is not seen as legitimate, which means that no one is investigating it except those who are determined to prove that it works. Those doing the therapy say they have a great success rate. But I remember a case where a big proponent for this therapy ended up in a gay bar after appearing on the cover of *Time* magazine with his legal wife, both of them claiming to have been cured and happily heterosexual. But there he was, the poster boy for reparative therapy, an icon of the anti-gay Christian far right, in a gay bar. In other words, a queer is a queer is a queer.

As for the grass always being greener, you're 16. Trust me, at 40 if someone asked me straight or gay, I'd take gay, thank you very much. My partner Andrew was the best thing that *ever* could have happened to me, and I wouldn't have wanted to miss him for the world. Also, I love not having the confines of society breathing down my neck as to what is a real "man." I love being able to be the "man" I want to be.

Yes, when Rosie O'Donnell was asked if she could choose straight or gay for her children, she said straight. That bothered me, because I think it sent a dangerous message, one you obviously received. But, in truth, who wouldn't make that choice for their children, given the climate in the U.S. and the rest of the world? No one wants their children to struggle and suffer and be treated as second-class citizens. But it is that climate that must change, not gays and lesbians.

What you are is a gift, not a curse. Always remember that.

No, homosexuality isn't "normal" statistically, but abnormal doesn't mean "wrong." Redheads are not normal. Left-handed people are not normal. And you are not normal. But you are not wrong. You are just living through a tumultuous time, one you will get through. Trust your heart and listen with your head. Your head knows what is logical. You are not an error, you are not a mistake—no more so than those redheads or left-handed people. You are, in fact, just the way nature intended. Enjoy your differences instead of wanting them changed. Stop worrying about being like "them" and just be like you. We need individuals in this world, not clones.

Always here if you want to talk.
Karel

Sixteen and wanting reparative therapy, what a shame! Yet it's a sentiment shared by many, young and old. Who among us hasn't thought for a moment that just for once they'd like to be accepted for who and what they are, and if they can't be, then they want to be like the rest, in the majority? It's not just the whining of a impetuous 16-year-old; it's a thought many gays and lesbians have, young or old.

And as I sit and examine the climate in this country—as my gay leaders say it's getting better and hold galas to pat themselves and those who cater to "us" on the back—a recent story about the Supreme Court blares in my head. It's 2002, and the court has recently announced that it is going to hear a case on the constitutionality of sodomy laws. Can you imagine? It's 2002—the highest court in the land has to rule on whether the state can regulate what goes on in a private bedroom between consenting adults. What's worse is that in 2002 anal and oral sex is still defined in some states as sodomy—abnormal sex. Nine states ban consensual sodomy for everyone: Alabama, Florida, Idaho, Louisiana, Mississippi, North Carolina, South Carolina, Utah, and Virginia. If that's not ridiculous enough, blatant homosexual discrimination on a state level is allowed in Texas, Kansas, Missouri, and Oklahoma, since they punish only homosexual sodomy.

And still, I wouldn't change a thing about who I am. My letter to Germany holds true.

Gays and lesbians have something so many others don't: a fundamental understanding about what love really, truly is, how it has to be fought for, how difficult it can be, and what an elusive prize it remains. Our partnerships don't come easily; we fight for them, fighting with society and often with each other. And we have an innate ability to form families—not traditional two-kids-and-the-dog type families, but extended families. Look around your queer holiday table—"the island of misfit toys"—as I once called it, and you'll see how the great despair and oppression we sometimes feel carve out a cavern that we then fill with love and joy, the love and joy of those related by blood and of those related by love.

Yes, my life may have been easier if I had been straight. I

wouldn't be having to answer ridiculous questions right now in my lawsuit over my partner's wrongful death if we could have been legally married. I wouldn't have to read in court papers *whereas Mr. Bouley is not an immediate family member under the law...* or have to prove that our domestic-partnership agreement matters. I wouldn't have to jump higher, run faster, and talk more carefully, always doing more than the other talk-show hosts, always having to prove I belong on mainstream radio, that my views are in fact valid—a struggle I face simply because I'm gay, and to the powers that be in radio, that means I have "listener hurdles" to cross.

But if I weren't gay I wouldn't have known the love of Andrew Howard, of Ken Pearson, of friends like Jason Young or Sean Devereaux, Emily Johnson or Karen Dittman...I wouldn't have known any of the life I hold dear because I wouldn't have been me. And I am gay, and no matter who may legislate against it, no matter how much I may question it, it has carved out my very soul, my essence. It has brought love and joy and marvelous friends with me now and many who have gone too soon. It has brought me face-to-face with devastating illness and shown me courage in so many ways that I never thought possible. It has shown me what life is really about. It has been a blessing—not a curse, an asset, not a flaw to be fixed.

There's so much in this world that needs to be repaired. Gays and lesbians are not on that list.

Why Isn't Mother's Day Enough?

I'm all for support groups. In today's I-must-understand-everything-I-do self-help world, you can't swing a dead cat without hitting a program for this or that malady, disorder, emotional distress, or special circumstance that needs support. And bless them one and all, a lot of coffee is consumed and a lot of meeting halls filled. But when the groups come out of the halls and begin marching down the street, I have a problem—well, with one in particular: PFLAG. There, I've said it. I've attacked the holy grail of the gay and lesbian community. The one organization that unilaterally brings parade-goers to their feet in support, the one organization that is seen as one of the most noble of all: PFLAG—Parents, Friends, and Family of Lesbians and Gays.

You see, I don't get it. I don't understand why I have to applaud someone for doing their job. No one applauds me daily for showing up for work, how about you? Each day, are you thanked for being a good worker? Or at home, for that matter, as a good brother, sister, father, mother, daughter, or son?

Now, I understand the premise of the organization: to give parents of gay children a place to go, to meet, to discuss their issues. That's all well and good. But I don't understand why I have to feel they are noble for accepting their gay children. Why are they doing something special? It is the parents' job to love their children; it is their duty, whether that child is gay or not, handicapped or not, rebellious or not, "A" student or "F." You don't see parents of leukemia patients or parents of cancer patients marching, getting standing ovations, so why parents of gays and lesbians? Aren't Mother's Day and Father's Day enough? Should white parents who adopt black babies march and say "I love my black child?"

Poppycock.

Yes, I know not every parent is accepting, but how about chastising those who aren't instead of overly rewarding those who are? Because nowadays, rewarding those who are sends a message that this is something extraordinary, something out of the norm, and that is a dangerous message indeed. Haven't we moved beyond "See, we're OK because our parents love us and we have straight friends"? That's the "friends" part of PFLAG, the straight friends. Oh, boy, we have parents and straight friends that love us—that must mean we're OK. Nonsense.

It's not that I want to do away with PFLAG. I do not. I know they're there to help some stone-age parents who still feel the worst thing that could happen in their family would be for a child to be gay. I would like to believe we are beyond that, but I know we are not. And there should be a place for those parents to turn. It's their deification by us, our community, that worries me. It plays to our lack of cultural self-esteem, and it's that innermost need to be validated by "them" that worries me. The glorification of those who accept us for who and what we are means that the converse is acceptable—that non-acceptance is in fact an option. We are allowing for that. And it is time that we move beyond that.

If you have a problem, it's your own. I'm not going to reward you for *not* having a problem with me or my sexuality, or anyone in my community. I'm not going to put you on a pedestal because you embrace your gay child. Ultimately, you shouldn't see me, him, her as your gay child but simply as your child who happens to be gay. And if you don't, you need the counseling as well as the support of PFLAG and other groups to get past that. But once you are past that, don't expect me or my community to reward you for your "right" thinking. It's like rewarding a thief for not stealing.

Now, I know this will be an unpopular opinion. But to progress, we must move beyond some things—just as I argue that blacks need to leave behind things like the NAACP. We can't even say the term "colored people" anymore in polite society, yet they continue to call the organization by that name. They want inclusion in the arts, yet hold their own awards that exclude whites, Asians, and Hispanics, either intentionally or by chance. I was told by Rick Callender, head of the NAACP's Silicon Valley office, that events like the NAACP Image Awards exist because blacks must recognize their own. They want integration into awards like the Oscars and the Emmys but then create a segregationist award ceremony—just like the GLAAD Media Awards are. If I'm in the arts, give me an Emmy, Grammy, Oscar, whatever. Don't single me out for my gay achievements; single me out for my overall achievements. GLAAD should rally for me to win one of those; the NAACP should throw its weight behind blacks in the areas where they wish to be represented.

Don't separate—the same goes for children and parents. Don't single me out as your gay child and then single yourself out because you accept me. I'm your child—it's your lot in life to accept and love me. If you're not up to that, you shouldn't have had children. And if you don't accept and love me, it's a testament to your intolerance, not to the fact that you deem me abnormal.

I was blessed with understanding parents. I know so many are not. And perhaps they are the ones who stand and cheer PFLAG. I understand that concept, but again, I feel it is time to move on and let PFLAG take its place among every other service organization, instead as one hailed as the most prestigious. I'm glad you love your gay son, but what made you think you had an option? His sexuality? Please. I'm happy you accept your lesbian daughter, but remove the word *lesbian* and she's still your daughter. That always should come first.

I'm glad PFLAG helps some parents regain the focus, the compass; that it is there to support those lost souls who believe otherwise. But for me, it is simply helping some play catch-up. Validation from anyone is no longer a requirement for us to exist in society as a whole because our existence is no longer up for debate, validation, vote, or approval, as far as I'm concerned. I'm used to that status. You should be too, as should my parents and yours. I don't feel a need to praise them or any straight people who call themselves "our" friends. Friends don't point out that I'm your friend in spite of our differences. True friends are those who don't notice the difference.

Bi-Curious or Gay Phobic?

I have always had trouble with the concept of bisexuality. Not that I've ever had any experience with it firsthand; I've always been gay, from day one. I missed the whole "coming out" process because for me it was never a question. You could turn out all the lights and put me in a room of 100 people and still spot me as the queer.

I did have a girlfriend in high school—we all did. I consider that my denial phase. I knew I was gay but didn't want to be because it just seemed hard; it seemed wrong. My girlfriend and I even had sex. That lasted a year, and then I started dating a fellow classmate, a male fellow classmate. It was no surprise to anyone—me, my parents, my classmates—although I must say it is the one thing I regret: My girlfriend's feelings ended up getting hurt, and I didn't want that. We discussed it all along, but matters of the heart know no logic. To this day she doesn't speak to me, and we live blocks apart. A bad ending, but one that had to end that way given that I was in fact gay.

And that's what perplexes me. As I look around today at the trend, the whole "bi-curious" thing, I can't help but wonder: Don't these people know that they will end up hurting themselves and others by not being completely honest? You see, I do not believe in bisexuality—pure, true bisexuality, at least not in the amount people claim. Now, my disbelief in it doesn't mean it doesn't exist, but in my experience it is a rarity indeed.

We all have a predilection for either men or women when it comes to sex, one way or the other, if we are honest with ourselves. And that's the hard part—honesty. Many men are afraid to say they want to experiment with other men because they fear it will label them gay, and socially that's a taboo, at least in many eyes. So many of these heterosexual men who want to play call themselves "bi" or "bi-curious."

Drawing lines in sexuality is a risky business because, historically, we have crossed those lines. Only in today's stringent society is it uncommon for men to have other men sexually, or women to have other women, yet maintain a heterosexual lifestyle. In many cultures throughout history it was not uncommon for either sex to have a same-sex lover and yet be considered heterosexual, because they were heterosexual at the core. I contend that having a same-sex lover does not make you gay. Being gay is so much more than sex—in fact, there can be gay celibates. It is a lifestyle, a way of living and thinking, a way of being. Men who enjoy sex with other men but maintain a heterosexual lifestyle are not bi, they are straight—because predominantly they interact sexually, emotionally, socially with women. The same goes for women who are married to men, have children, and then find themselves having a fling with a female lover. They are not bi, they are heterosexual at the core, but with an exploring mind.

We all know one of these. I do, or did—a totally heterosexual neo-Nazi skinhead who loved to come over every so often and play with the boys. Was he gay? Nope. Was he bi? Nope. He was very, very heterosexual but not sexually limited. He enjoyed sex, period.

Calling oneself bisexual is sexual ambivalence, and I find it hard to believe that such indecision exists in nature. The problem is labels. Cross one line and you get a new label, so people that want broader sexual experiences create a new, kinder, gentler label. Being called bi is in no way as stigmatizing as being called gay.

The label *bisexual* is also a cop-out for those who are predominantly gay but may at times have sexual encounters with opposite-sex partners. It allows them a cushion, a safety zone. They never have to really face the fact that they are in fact gay, because they have this preconceived notion: *Sometimes I sleep with people of the opposite sex, but I'm not "totally" gay so I must be bi.* No, you're not bi, just homophobic. You think that being called gay is awful and that by labeling yourself bi you are removing a harsh stigma.

Say it with me: poppycock.

Ultimately, in your heart and soul, you know which sex you prefer, which sexual orientation you identify as, gay or not. To create a third class of sexuality only confuses the matter more and again allows a comforting cushion between you and the homophobic world around you. Well, cushions are for sofas. Fess up to who you are, one way or another, and then live with it. That doesn't mean you have to be limited. I'd like to see a time when all labels are removed from sexuality, period. Where normal sexuality is eliminated, meaning that each person decides what is normal for him or her without any classification at all. Romans did it. Many Latin cultures do it. Our puritanical selves should abandon an ideology of limitations when it comes to something as wonderful as sexuality. But until we do, have the courage to at least choose sides.

Why? Because You Set Yourself Up

I love doing my radio show. There's no two ways about it. It's one of the few jobs I've ever had where I leave more hyped up than when I got there. Of course, that can be a curse when I travel. Recently, I was in San Francisco (where my station is) to do the show from there. Since I live in Los Angeles, this, of course, meant staying at a hotel. So after the show I was sitting, amped up and ready to go, at the lovely Hotel Mosser. Me, a 19-inch TV, and pay-per-view.

Back at the hotel I reached into my backpack, pulled out my Apple PowerBook, and logged on. What do you know, there's my old friend Larry Flick, back at his home in New York. Larry's into the bear scene—a lot—and quickly suggested I leave the confines of my room and venture out to the Lone Star. The people will be friendly, he assured me, I'd be comfortable, it was close by, and it beat watching Vin Diesel one more time.

I don't really do bars alone, even when traveling, but I figured, well, why not? Maybe it would be interesting. So I donned a fabulous coat and scarf to walk almost two miles to the club, being too cheap to take a taxi and being assured by the front desk that it was within walking distance. I didn't realize Susan Powter had a night job at the Mosser.

When I arrived I found a dimly lit bear bar with an even darker patio (which I avoided) and strange substances on the floor near the bathroom. I don't drink anymore, so I ordered a club soda and ended up with a Perrier. That's fine.

Five minutes there I realized why Larry thought I would feel comfortable: Almost everyone there had at least 20% body fat. *Great,* I thought, *Larry sees me as large,* but that's another column. The funny thing was, those who didn't have 20%-plus body fat seemed to be looking for others like them despite this being a bar filled with just the opposite. It made for great people-watching.

Soon a nice gentleman named Jesus began talking with me—not because he was particularly interested but because I was seated at the bar and the room was about to overflow, so he and his friends were literally in my face.

After talking for a few moments I asked why his friend looked so upset. His friend was a very attractive man, certainly not a "bear" by most standards, but he had the look: tight jeans, which he fit beautifully; plaid shirt; scruffy, unshaved face; sandy blond hair. He was right out of an Eddie Bauer catalog.

Jesus replied that his friend was upset because someone had "groped" him, and he felt it inappropriate. I laughed, openly. Then the angry friend asked, "What's so funny?" I asked him if he was seriously upset that someone fondled him. He said yes, he was, and he wanted an apology from the guy. I laughed again. Then the talk-show host in me, the amped-up one, took over.

I looked at this fine specimen of a man and asked what, exactly, was he doing here? We were in a dimly lit bear bar on a Saturday night in a less-than-classy part of town. We weren't at a GLAAD gathering, or even the Ritz or an upscale local club like Ruby Sky. We were on a side street next to a freeway near midnight. He was dressed in tight jeans, filling them out nicely. He had a 1987 quarter in his pocket, or so I could read through the fabric. His shirt was open enough to reveal a nice chest, firm and just hairy enough. It happened on a patio where one would need night-vision goggles to adequately order a drink. What the hell did he expect?

His reply was that no one has the right to invade your space in such a personal way, no matter where you are.

Say it with me: poppycock.

I am sick to death of people like him, people who put themselves in situations where the outcome could only be one thing, and then getting upset when it happens. I began to lecture him, not that he wanted to hear it, but somebody had to set this guy straight, so to speak.

For years this has been a peeve of mine. When I heard about the Mike Tyson rape case, I wondered, What was a woman doing with a drunk boxer, in bed, naked, and then saying no? Didn't she know that going to a hotel room with someone three times your size while drinking and getting naked isn't a good idea?

Did she deserve to be raped? No, but we don't live in a perfect world, and people tend to forget that.

The same with Matthew Shepard. For years Andrew and I came under attack on radio because we simply asked what was he doing in that truck, at that time, with those people? Not a good idea at all.

What part of *hot coffee* didn't the woman understand as she drove through McDonald's and then placed it between her legs? Not a good idea to place a hot beverage there while driving. Yet she got millions from Ronald.

There is an epidemic in America of shirking personal responsibility. Countless times we put ourselves in situations that could go badly, and when they do we scream about the injustice of it all. We make ourselves professional victims, and it's a crying shame.

Gays and lesbians do it more often than their nongay counterparts, or so it would appear. That, of course, is based on my own nonscientific personal research, but it appears true nonetheless.

For instance, Andrew and I once had to meet friends at Cook's Corner in Trabuco Canyon, Calif. It's a world-famous biker bar in the middle of a canyon—not filled with your weekend warriors but real live bikers. On weekends it can have over 1,000 people there.

We were driving a little Nissan Sentra at the time. On the back windshield was a pink triangle emblem. It had always bothered Andrew; he didn't feel our car needed to tell people which sex we slept with. After all, outside of those annoying, cheesy girls on mudflaps of trucks, who really does that anymore? Straight men don't run around with stickers saying I LIKE VAGINA. Or most of them don't, anyway.

In any event, as we approached the bar, many of the passing bikers, with their well-matched women on the backs of their bikes, scowled at our car. We knew why.

When we arrived, we were uncomfortable waiting for our friends in our vehicle. So I got out and took the triangle off that window. It shocked Andrew. I had fought for that thing for so long. But suddenly I didn't need it anymore. After all, each day he and I went on radio and were an openly gay couple in front of millions of listeners. I no longer needed my car to tell people about my sexual orientation. And besides, it was putting us in real, perceptible danger.

Now, should I have had to do that to feel safe? No. The bikers should have just accepted us. And then we all should have joined hands and sung "Kumbaya." The fact is, though, taking down the sticker made us safer. It removed something that might have been an irritant at this kind of establishment.

We weren't going to be victims because of something we could prevent.

Cop-out? Maybe in some people's eyes. But to me it's just reality.

The reality is, if you go into a dark bear bar in San Francisco on a Saturday night looking very fine, someone may grab you in an inappropriate area without your consent. The reality is, if you crawl into bed with someone, drunk and naked, who's bigger than you and expecting sex, they may not take "no" for an answer. The reality is, if you get into a car with strangers in a small town of close-minded people, you may end up beaten and tied to a fence post. Those are harsh facts, and ones we all know in our hearts. Yet ones we ignore.

We are responsible for what happens to us. I realize that, because I am a media figure, I have put myself at risk for some wacko who disagrees with me to hurt me. I have a security system at home, and when I do personal appearances the station requires armed guards be with me (or any of the hosts). Should I be hurt for voicing my opinions? Nope, but chances are one day I might be. If I don't like that thought, I should be a banker.

The same goes for HIV. I have maintained that for any gay man who contracts HIV in 2003, it's his own damn fault. Am I glad gay men get HIV and AIDS? Of course not. It's a tragedy. But the information about how to avoid infection has been out there for almost two decades. Even children know about it now. We gay men certainly know how it's spread.

Ignorance is not an excuse for shirking personal responsibility. If you are going to have sex, you should be prepared. Be responsible. If not, you only have yourself to blame for the outcome. Not "Oh, they didn't tell me..." Not "Oh, I thought we were monogamous and he was negative..." Foolish. I don't care if you've been married to the guy for nearly 12 years, you should still use a condom every single time. Your health isn't something you should be willing to bet any man's fidelity on. Men, at times, are pigs. And pigs can't always be trusted at a buffet. So it's wise to protect yourself no matter how much you trust your partner. And if you don't, it's your fault, not your partner's, if you turn up positive.

I realize this concept of personal responsibility is foreign to most Americans. Our courts are filled with case after case of people suing someone for the stupidest things, things they should have seen coming or things they put themselves at risk for and then, when the worst happened, tried to blame someone else for.

Why? Because no one wants that kind of responsibility anymore. No one wants to feel that they could have actually brought about some kind of harm to themselves. *It had to be someone else's fault. At least partly. I couldn't possibly be responsible.*

This also applies to the fight for gay rights. We need to own up to the fact that we are so far behind in this country (Can we marry? Can we openly serve in he military? Can we even have gay sex legally in every state? No. No. No.) because we have been a disorganized movement at best. We don't have a real leader, like a Gandhi, a King. We give those who would limit our rights all the ammunition they need to point out we are deviants (just watch *Queer as Folk*).

We demand and expect so much from others without demanding or expecting a lot from ourselves. We share the blame for our nonacceptance. We've tolerated it for so long and haven't changed a lot as a culture to try and gain it. Well, on second thought, we've changed but not always for the better. Each of us who isn't out at work and home, doesn't stay an informed voter, engages in promiscuous sex, joins the drug culture—we each play a part in our own repression.

It is, in fact, partially our fault. When we take responsibility for that, things will change.

I started walking back to the hotel shortly after my

encounter at the Lone Star. When I got to the hotel, I realized I had been a gay man, alone, in a fabulous coat, jamming to the latest Anastacia album playing on the iPod in my pocket, walking through parts of town that I had no idea about as far as safety.

Had I been mugged, it would have been my fault for being so stupid and not asking the best way home or calling a taxi.

And as I walked into the Mel's Diner near the hotel at 1:30 A.M. and ordered a cheeseburger and fries (I hadn't eaten since lunch) I realized that when I lie clutching my chest in 30 or 40 years, that too will be my fault. I won't sue Mel's for making me fat.

But that burger and fries sure tasted good at that moment. And in today's world the moment is really all that counts. Most of us seem to feel it's all we have.

Just remember: You, me, everyone—we are responsible for what happens to us in that moment, good or bad.

Who's SAR-ry Now?

I never thought I'd say it, but I approve of Bush. Well, let me rephrase: King George II has finally done something of which I approve. On Friday, April 4, 2003, he added SARS—severe acute respiratory syndrome—to the list of diseases that can call for a patient to be quarantined. The executive order, which allows for "detainment or quarantine" of people infected with SARS, is the first of its kind in 20 years. And the last disease to be added to the quarantine list was the Ebola virus. That's the one that causes you to bleed to death through every orifice of your body, including your eyes, and it has a fatality rate of more than 50%. There's no treatment.

SARS is a severe viral pneumonia. There's no treatment except supportive measures. Compared with Ebola, it has a much lower—but still very scary—death rate. Most people recover, but some, especially older people or others with health problems, can't fight it off, and succumb in a matter of days.

Of course, there's no need to worry yet about massive quarantines. The last time anyone was detained in federal quarantine was 1963, to prevent the spread of smallpox. But at least this is being addressed early in the game—unlike the last deadly virus to come around in the early 1980s, HIV. Where were the executive orders then, the lead from the Centers for Disease Control (before it added "and Prevention" to its name) or the World Health Organization? Where was the government outcry, the immediate worldwide involvement?

Nowhere. Because just queers were dying.

I'd like to think this response to SARS from the Administration is one brought about by years of learning from the mistakes of how HIV was handled. Alas, I doubt that's the case.

SARS swept the world by storm in March and April after first appearing in China in November 2002. (China later apologized for not letting everyone else know a little sooner— oops!) Everyone began wearing masks in Hong Kong and Beijing, where the disease appears to have originated. People on planes complaining of flu-like symptoms or fevers of 100.4 degrees or higher caused entire planes to be quarantined on runways until safety was assured. Because the respiratory ailment could be fatal, reaction was swift.

What's eerie is that statements from the CDC and WHO could easily have been confused for statements about HIV 20 years ago. "We don't know the exact cause yet, but it is believed..." "We're not 100% sure of the way it is transmitted, but it appears to be..." "We know the disease can be fatal..." "This virus appears to spread rapidly, and we don't know very much about the epidemiology..."

As I watched *And the Band Played On*—the HBO film that chronicles the bungling of the early years of the AIDS epidemic—on late-night television in the middle of all of this, I wondered what would it have been like if HIV had really been treated as a disease, and not a political or social condition.

In 1982 they were arguing in San Francisco whether to close the bathhouses. At that time, my late husband Andrew was 16 years old. What if they had closed the bathhouses? Quarantined those with HIV or at least those with clear symptoms of AIDS until they could figure this out? Would Andrew, my dear friend Lorenzo, Michael Mungarro, John Delicce, Frederick, Mark Rodgers (insert other names here)... Would they all still be here now if Reagan had issued executive orders, if the gay community had shut their mouths and let the CDC work with impunity in the community? I'd like to have at least seen what would have happened. They did finally close the bathhouses in 1985, but they reopened shortly thereafter. And now they are back and as popular ever.

What am I suggesting? That the government should have rounded up all the gays and tested them in the early days, as soon as the antibody test became available? Quarantine those found to be infected? Mandatory reporting of all sex partners? Well, maybe, if that's what needs to be done for viruses that kill people, spread like wildfire, and go on to decimate the world and an entire generation of gay men, not to mention Africans and Asians and...so many dead. Maybe such extreme measures would not have been necessary; I'm not a medical expert. But no matter what needed to be done, HIV should have been treated like a fatal communicable virus, just like SARS is being treated, just like any deadly agent of infection—it should have been handled however the medical experts deemed best, not the politicians, not the shouting homos crying out that their rights were being violated, not a generation painted as victims, not the civic leaders, not the businesspeople, not talk-show hosts or writers like me—none of them.

The people in charge should have been the doctors, the virologists, the experts in the handling of a communicable infectious disease. What they said we should do, we should have done.

But SARS was and is different, you might say, because it's airborne. Unlike HIV, SARS can be caught from a cough or even passing touch. Yes, HIV was sexually transmitted, for the most part. But we didn't know that at first. Some even thought HIV was airborne early on. But HIV wasn't airborne; it proved to be an STD. So it should have been treated like one. For most STDs, diagnosis mandates the notification of sexual partners. Not HIV. With HIV, no one could be contacted because anonymity was demanded, the right to privacy invoked. For some reason it was a special STD. The reason? The gay community's protest fell in line with the stigma and the fear from every side.

It was too scary, too shameful. No one wanted to know.

I've heard all the arguments that measures like mandatory testing, possible quarantine, mandatory notification of partners and such would have pushed those suspected of having HIV underground. Well, let's look at what the converse did—the secrecy, the anonymity. How many dead? Over half a million in the United States alone as of 2002 and millions—almost an entire continent—worldwide. Monetary cost? Hundreds of billions. And in the past 20 years, did we find a cure to make it all better, to salve our guilt for letting it spread unchecked? Nope. We have partially effective treatments, some almost as deadly as the disease, and not so much as a potential vaccine, much less one that works.

Yes, our community, who screamed for our sexual freedom, got to continue having sex however we wanted. I've always argued that anyone who has unprotected sex and is HIV-positive is committing a criminal act and, if it can be proved as such, should be prosecuted for assault and battery. If someone had smallpox and knowingly went around infecting people, they'd be treated like a criminal, right? If someone who knew they had SARS decided to hop into a crowded bus or airplane and cough on everyone, wouldn't they be dragged away in handcuffs and quarantined? Oh, but not HIV: Today we have parties in bigger cities where people actually go to have sex with HIV-positive people: bug-chasing parties. It's criminal.

While I hold the Reagan administration, the CDC, and WHO to blame, I also shoulder a part of that blame as part of the gay community. We behaved so badly—still do, when it comes to AIDS. Our sexual freedom was worth all those lives, right? And what freedom was that, again? Because no one except the lunatic right ever suggested gay men stop having sex. They suggested we stop having unprotected sex. They suggested we should stop having sex in ways and places that put people at risk for infection. But no, even that was an infringement. The sexual freedom of the few hundred or thousands of gay men at the beginning who could have been legally forced—yes, even via quarantine—to stop spreading this disease in America, that was more important than the lives of millions of others. It was more horrible to consider exactly the kinds of travel restrictions and mandatory testing of immigrants that we're all supporting with SARS than it was to protect the hundreds of thousands of our gay brothers who would contract HIV and die.

All those steps at the beginning that are now being taken with SARS and could have been taken with HIV weren't, because AIDS took hold in an already oppressed community, one that the far right would have been happy to toss into internment camps with or without a deadly disease as an excuse. I understand what happened—I just can't figure out why. It's a virus. It's a medical condition. But we made it into a social condition, a political issue. Now it's buried in politics and red ribbons, and advertisements seem to tell us that it's chic, as slick ads with buff men reassure us that we can live with HIV no problem—don't worry about changing our lives. It's Magic Johnson time.

Perhaps the hoopla and early intervention in the case of SARS will stop this new infection. Who knows with a disease? Maybe extreme efforts at the beginning wouldn't have helped stop HIV. We'll never know. Even now, we treat HIV like a stigma, not a virus. We don't report those with it to any central medical authority; we don't notify their partners. We don't have mandatory testing for those at risk. In some places, if a doctor is stuck by a needle accidentally, they can't even demand to test for HIV the blood of the person that the needle was in first. How ridiculous is that? Every other infectious, incurable disease has been treated differently, from Ebola to SARS.

As I look back on the last 20-plus years, I do see progress. Andrew lived most of his adult life with HIV thanks to new treatments. He died of what I allege is malpractice, not AIDS. He lived 13 years with it, and that's something.

But I also see so many mistakes. Made then, being made now—and I cry. Literally. That sappy movie *And the Band Played On,* a bad film by some accounts, made me cry for hours. I've been grieving every two years for the past 20 years. And I've had the easy part—I've stayed behind. Tears are a luxury of the living. Angry? You bet I'm angry. At myself, at the gay community, at the Reagan administration; I'm even mad at the current Bush administration for its swift action in SARS, because there was so little action against HIV. I'm angry because of all the goodbyes.

And I'm angry that the mystery never will be solved as to whether it would have changed anything to treat HIV as the deadly virus it is, like SARS, and not as a social or political condition. I'll never know if all those people really had to die, or if the religious right would have gotten their wish and all the gays in the U.S. would be in a big camp in Montana somewhere. Well, never fear; if we were, I'm sure Jeffrey Sanker would be there to throw the annual White Party, given all the snow. There'd still be lots of unprotected sex because they'd think "Hell, we're all in this stupid AIDS camp anyway. I'm sure there'd be alcohol, and maybe even drugs other than AZT, protease inhibitors, etc., you know, E, X, K, because we'd all be in one place…how easy to distribute." Wait, this sounds like Palm

Springs, West Hollywood, San Francisco...maybe they all got their wish after all.

SARS is a virus that can kill. HIV is a virus that can kill. To a virologist, they're the same in that they need to find the cause, find a treatment, and find a cure. They need to isolate them and contain them. They need to prevent them. Each is unique, yet much of the methodology is the same. But oh, to the people, how they're so very different. To the people, SARS is a health threat wildly spreading while AIDS was, and is, an indictment on a culture. In this tale of two viruses there is no happy ending, but at least SARS has a better beginning.

Speeding Things Up

I remember the scene vividly. It was the mid '90s. I was at my best friend Lorenzo's memorial. My husband Andrew was by my side. I was devastated. Lorenzo and I were so close for so many years.

A year earlier we had been in Hawaii together, all of us. We came back, and he rapidly got ill from his HIV: Kaposi's, PCP, CMV, one after the next. Then the inevitable. I was there, through it all, even at the end.

After the memorial I was out front, trying to find my way, literally. I had forgotten where the car was. Andrew came to me, led me. We bumped into a friend of Lorenzo's. One of his "party" friends. Lorenzo was beautiful, muscled, handsome, loved to go dancing. This friend offered us some crystal meth, in memory of Lorenzo. I stood there, mouth open. I knew this person was HIV-positive as well. All I could say was, "It's called speed, you idiot. That means it speeds everything up. Do you want to speed up your virus, speed up the amount of time you have left—"

"But Lorenzo loved it, we just did some a week ago..."

Poor stupid man. And, poor, stupid Lorenzo.

Through my columns at Advocate.com and other places I've taken a lot of hits from people who blast me for my stance on drug usage in the gay community. And now I'm supposed to be surprised by a study quoted in the *San Francisco Chronicle* recently repeating a report from health experts that up to 40% of gay men in San Francisco have used crystal meth and that 25–30% of patients at one local clinic who were newly infected with HIV reported using meth during the previous six months.

Michael Siever, director of the Stonewall Project, a speed recovery program at the University of California, San Francisco, was quoted by the *Chronicle* in May 2003 as saying, "It's the perfect drug for gay men. What else allows you to party all night long, whether you're dancing or having sex?"

And that's what we all want to do, right? Party all night long, dance, have sex. So of course we need the perfect drug for it. And it seems we've found it, in alarming numbers.

Other recent stories have stated that those who use meth increase their risk of HIV infection by 50%.

Poor stupid gay men.

I suppose the same goes for alcohol and our nongay counterparts. I have always contended that the world would have a lot fewer new babies if alcohol weren't around. Men and women get drunk, have sex, get pregnant. Maybe if you're straight and drink around the opposite sex your chances of getting pregnant (or getting someone pregnant) are 50% higher than for people who don't drink. I don't have a study to back that up, but it makes sense.

And that's why I didn't need the San Francisco study to tell me what I already know: If you use meth, you're more likely to get HIV. Again, it makes sense. And thanks to stories like those in the *San Francisco Chronicle* and now in the *Los Angeles Times* and *The New York Times,* it just shows our nongay counterparts that many of us don't have any—sense, that is.

Maybe I'm supposed to feel compassion for these people who turn to drugs for fun. I mean, we all do, legal or otherwise. Got pain? Get Vicodin. Got troubles? Have a Bud. Need to have fun? Absolut-ly have some. Down and out? Xanax is your friend. Kid acting up? Ritalin your troubles away. Face it, we're a drug culture. Myself included.

While I may not drink alcohol regularly any longer, make no mistake: When the days get too hard, the grief too much over the loss of my partner, the crying overwhelming, I take a Xanax. Granted, I've got over 300 Xanax in the house because my doctors have been giving them to me for two years now, and I take about two a month total. But they're there. And if my back hurts too much and I cannot move out of bed, I reach for the Soma and Vicodin so I can function. Because I refuse to have surgery. No, I'm no saint. I take drugs. Legal ones, and as prescribed, but I take them. I wish I could abuse them, I do. The problem is, I need them for their real purpose. But meth...what real purpose does that have? Life enhancement? Please, life is real enough, who needs it sped up?

Yet I simply cannot feel anything but a overwhelming sense of "Oh well..." even for my dearly departed Lorenzo. I was so angry when I found out about his meth use. I knew he did some when he partied. But after Hawaii, after he came back and was getting sick, how could he? And how could anyone use it with him, seeing his state? Those are real friends, I tell ya. Every gay man who does meth with another gay man is a real friend indeed. Lorenzo didn't do it in front of me when he was ill. He knew I would have had his ass about it. I wouldn't have stood for it. He would have had to choose: me in his life helping him through his final days, or meth. Because I refuse to help idiots. So he hid it. Who was the idiot there?

You know, I'm not really worried about those of you out there who do it. If you want to, do it, and die, or pay whatever consequences come along, including increased risk for

HIV—go right ahead. No, I am not really worried about you. I'm more concerned for what you're doing to me.

In the past two weeks there have been major stories in major newspapers from major health officials warning about major health risks that gay men pose to themselves and to the world as a whole. First, there was the warning from L.A. County officials about the spread of syphilis surrounding the annual White Party on Easter weekend, because Palm Springs, the gay mecca that hosts the White Party, is the syphilis capital of California. Newspapers from coast to coast ran stories about the party known for "drugs, sex, and music" as *The New York Times* put it, and how gay men are wantonly spreading syphilis and God knows what else. While doing radio in Palm Springs as a guest host, I had to answer a caller's question as to why their 12-year-old needed to see a six-foot cock with a safer-sex message on it, running down the street being chased by little syphilis-sore characters. I had no answer. And now, this story.

Look, you want to kill yourselves, fine. You want to do it all in the name of partying, the circuit, the fact that drugs help you feel better about yourself because the world doesn't accept you, whatever, it's fine with me, do it. But when you start doing it and then the rest of the world thinks that we all are doing it, that's where I have a problem. Can't you be a fuck-up in private?

So now the world has more ammo. They now know that we go to Palm Springs to dance and have sex and spread disease. They all know that many of us do meth, have sex, and spread disease. They'll dismiss it, because after all, we're just killing ourselves. But you see, that's why I can't dismiss it. Don't you get it? *We're killing ourselves.* Those engaging in the behavior are dying, literally, and those who aren't are being killed socially by the stigma of those who are.

I keep saying that many gay men need to grow up. Well, it looks like many may of them never make it out of adoles-

cence. It's 2003 and we still don't know how to take care of
ourselves. As we enter the season of Pride, I'm sure I'll see
more stories about the many health risks we pose to ourselves, the risks we take on. Boy, we've got a lot to be proud
of. I can't wait to see what the *Chronicle* or *Times* runs in a
few weeks. GAY MEN ON METH TAKE TO STREETS TO CELE-
BRATE PRIDE AND DISEASE across the land—DJ POOPY-POO TO
SPIN AND NAMELESS DISCO DIVA TO PERFORM. That's not you,
you say? Too bad—who's going to know the difference?
There are enough of them for you to share the banner. You
don't like it? Then speak up. You see, if we don't start clean-
ing up from within, there won't be much left to monitor.

Viva La Men

"You're a very funny, happy person. Why do you write so much about the bad and not the good?"

I'm at cocktails with my longtime friend Thea Austin, the artist Karen Dittman, and my biologist roommate, Sean Devereaux, and the subject of my Advocate.com columns has come up. Thea, who asked the above question, is not gay, but performs a lot in the gay community—she's a singer for Pusaka, Thunderpuss, Snap!, and SoulSearcher.

Then my friend Karen looks across the table and says, "For the next five minutes, you are to say only good things about being gay. After all, the word *gay* means *happy*!"

I fall silent. The TV at Acapulco restaurant talks of reaction to the news from San Francisco about the rampant use of crystal meth among gay men. I remain silent. And I think.

Truth be told, I love being gay and have written about that love many times—but not recently. So I sit, time ticking, and wrack my brain for something nice to say about the gay community.

Thea says, "I'm performing this weekend at Gay Pride in Long Beach. That's a good event, isn't it?"

Well, I don't want to hand her my "Ashamed of Pride" article.

Ticking...ticking...

"Sean!" I blurt. Everyone, including my roommate, looks at me.

"What?"

"Sean is a positive thing about being gay."

Let me explain. I love gay men. I simply do, not just sexually but all around. I love gay men. Butch ones. Fem ones. Fat, loud ones. Skinny, buff ones. I love gay men, particularly as friends and roommates. All people should have a gay man in their life.

Take Sean, for instance. He's a biologist, the only openly gay biologist working at the Long Beach Aquarium of the Pacific. He loves his job, even though he's had to endure the word *fag* being written on his locker not once but four times. When a baby puffin hatched near midnight one evening, Sean was paged, and we left a local club and rushed to the aquarium. Tears welled up in his eyes when he saw the little featherless thing.

Sean delights in finding a new species of this or that orchid or succulent. He makes me stop to smell flowers all the time, his favorite being freesia. He introduces me to his friends at the aquarium without shame or apprehension, not worried about how they're going to handle a loudmouth talk-show host who is gay from the get-go. He'll spend an hour online researching how to find shortcuts to his favorite PS2 game while whipping up chicken paprikash in the kitchen. He shaves his head into a pseudo-mohawk—a faux-hawk, if you will—and has a pointed goatee that often gets a tug from his friends.

He is a big homo. And the best friend a person could have.

He laments over not being able to get a date and complains about how he doesn't like gay bars while on his way to one. He is out and proud at work but thinks gay Pride festivals miss the point. He treats Home Depot like it's

Disneyland and glows openly when he can go to H&H Nursery in Long Beach.

And when the world gets too much for me, he's there, trying to make me laugh or running out for Del Taco and a DVD so we can sit in the TV room and forget about being single. He's the guy who's brimming with delight about going with his mother on a PartyLite cruise and being trapped on a boat with thousands of women who have sold enough candles through in-home parties to get to the Bahamas.

Sean is a gay man, and I love him. I love him because gay men are so wonderful to love. If there were a typical gay man—and I don't think there is—I would want that man to be Sean. Yes, there are those in our midst who are self-destructive, who make headlines, who appear to have only 12 brain cells left. But I believe they are not the norm. The norm is the gay couple Sean and I encounter while grocery shopping: both of them pumped up, one in sweats with "1892" across the butt (what's that about? I've seen it twice). They were arguing over what to bring to a Mother's Day brunch. The norm is the gay male nurse I'm interviewing to be my mom's home health care worker; he works part-time as a nurse, does in-home support services, lives with a roommate, and is working toward a degree in health care.

Everyone should have a gay male friend or roommate in their life. No one else will be able to make you laugh, cry, or wonder; no one else will make you want to hug him one minute then shake your head at him the next. Who else (outside of Ryan Seacrest) will spend five minutes deciding which hair gel is best from the five he has in the medicine cabinet? Who else will know what movie to see or what play is hot right now? Who else will know everything going on in the neighborhood? No one else, at least not to the degree of a gay male friend or roommate.

I love gay men because they survive and thrive. They take what society has thrown at them and learn how to adapt.

Most gay men had to develop a sense of self early on in life because they had no role models, no outside guidance to help shape who they are as a person. They had to figure it out for themselves, and most developed a unique and wonderful style of existence. That's why some are secure enough to work 9 to 5 and then come home and throw on heels and a wig and do Cher at the local club. They're able to cross lines quickly and effortlessly, because growing up, they felt already on the out-side of what was normal. Gay men got to, and get to, rede-fine what it is to be a normal man. They get to incorporate things masculine and things feminine all in one—caring with strength, compassion with male arrogance, blatant sexuality with the need for emotional connection—all wrapped up in a package that is usually far more put-together than that of their heterosexual counterparts.

Yes, I love gay men. And I love being a gay male. It has helped me more than I'll ever know. If I weren't gay, I would have never been able to love someone like my late husband, Andrew Howard. What a great gay man he was—writer, cook, gardener, philosopher, talk-show host, historian, bitchy queen, and masculine nature guy. He could put shoes on a horse, ski down a treacherous slope, and then come home and pick color swatches for the living room while creating some-thing fabulous in the kitchen. He could be a tender lover or an out-and-out pig. He was a wonderful gay man indeed. And if I weren't gay, I never would have been able to be intimate with him, and that would have been a tragic shame.

It sounds stupid. It sounds silly. But when I think of something positive I like about the community, it goes back to my very essence, the very core part of who I am—men, gay men.

And maybe that's where it all starts for all of us. Maybe we should strip down the politics, the Pride, the hype and hoopla and remember what it is we love most, why we're fighting the battles, why we're trying to win the war. Being gay has been so politicized, so scrutinized, so sterilized at times that many forget what being gay is all about.

For me, at its core, being gay is about loving men—I mean, really, truly loving gay men, all of them, for all their foibles and triumphs. It's not about AB 25 or Sen. Rick Santorum; it's not about Log Cabin Republican clubs or the White Party. It's about men, and thank God, Allah, Buddha, and whoever else that there are still so many wonderful gay men out there in the world to love--from Andrew to Sean to those I've yet to meet.

The next time I'm down on the community, feeling torn about who and what I am, all I need to do is look around at my circle of friends, take a walk through a Home Depot or grocery store, pop into a museum or the local A Different Light bookstore and take it all in. Gay men are the bomb, and being one of them is a blessing, not a condition, a fun adventure, not an internment.

The Million-Dollar Question

Progress is all around us, from my new Handspring Treo 300—which is a Palm Pilot, mobile phone, instant messenger, and Star Trek telecommunicator all in one—to the airport on my laptop, which allows me to beam this column wirelessly to my editor at *The Advocate* without leaving my sofa or local coffeehouse. Technology is amazing, and medicine is keeping us alive longer—improving quality of life and quantity. We even have smart bombs that make war kinder, gentler, more accurate.

Yes, progress is everywhere—except in our social collective. Socially, much of the country (much of the world, for that matter) is still in the Stone Age. While Texas does everything it can to make—and this is a quote from a lawmaker—abortion "impossible, if not illegal," it took the Supreme Court until mid 2003 to decide that so-called sodomy is all right between consenting adults.

Yes, we are in the dark ages in some areas. That's why it's no surprise that today, the million-dollar question for public figures isn't whether they have ever killed someone, cheated, stole, or bribed.. Oh, no, today's million-dollar question, for politician or entertainer, is "Are you gay?"

That question has come up very publicly in the recent past. First, there was the case of U.S. representative Mark Foley of Florida, who called a press conference recently to denounce journalists who were reporting that Foley is well-known around his Florida district to be gay. Foley, you see, is seeking the Republican nomination for one of Florida's U.S. Senate seats. The five-term congressman refused to address directly any questions about his sexuality at the press conference he called to denounce the rumors—he wasn't there to say that they weren't true; he was there to say that it was nobody's business but his. The rumors, he alleged, were part of a smear campaign by Democratic opponents. (Later it turned out that the chief culprit in sending out copies of the offending article was a staff member of one of Foley's Republican colleagues.)

I had to laugh—a smear campaign? Maybe it's just me, but a smear campaign in politics would be more likened to allegations that he stole funds, lied under oath, received fraudulent votes, or some other such underhanded doings. But oh, no, in Florida—and in the United States, apparently—allegations of homosexuality far outweigh any other such accusations. Drown someone under a bridge on the East Coast? We can forgive that. But sleep with a man? No way.

A few weeks later *American Idol* runner-up Clay Aiken was asked an obvious question at a press conference: How do you feel about the fact that many of your fans are gay and assume that you are too? Clay dodged the question by ignoring it. He could have copped out, à la Robbie Williams, and said, "I'm whatever the fans want me to be." He could have denied it. Hell, he could have just said, like Foley, "It's none of your damned business." But no, he just moved on, a move some see as a lie by omission. Certainly an evasion.

So what's the big deal?

There can be no doubt that sexuality is magnified in the realms of celebrity and politics. And that, it seems, makes coming out such a momentous occasion that some people would rather skip it altogether, no matter how openly gay they may be around town (which is reportedly the case with Foley). George Michael hid his true sexuality for years, and had it not been for that arrest in a Beverly Hills bathroom, he might never have officially come out. Rosie O'Donnell waited until she retired from her daytime TV show to find her yellow and embrace the pink publicly.

Tom Cruise, who says he's not gay (and says it and says it and says it), received a multimillion-dollar settlement because of those haunting gay allegations.

It's true, when you're out and in the public eye that *gay* can become your first name. I'm the gay talk-show host on KGO AM 810 San Francisco; no matter what I do, that's me. And that's the fear. Famous people and politicians don't want "gay" to overtake who and what they're about.

Problem is, inquiring minds want to know.

And that's where our backward social views come into play. In a perfect world, it shouldn't matter. But it does matter. Because, like it or not, being seen as gay is still being seen as damaged goods, second-class, third-rate. With the gay moniker comes a host of preconceived notions about who and what the person is.

We don't do anything to help any of these people with their decisions to stay in or to come out. As America sees images like those on the popular *Queer as Folk* glorified and praised by the queer community, can you blame Clay for not wanting to be associated with that same community? He's trying to sell records to kids in trailer parks, not those on their way to a Babylon after-hours party. As for Foley, he's running in a Bible Belt–brimmed state, one that wishes South Beach would fall off and become part of Cuba. Not likely he wants to be associated with what the modern-day gay image has become. Can you see it? A news story on Miami Pride, showing drag queens and dykes on bikes and then "in other related news, gay candidate Foley..." Oh, yeah, that's a winning strategy.

But while I understand it, I don't condone it. Only the most self-loathing gay person would treat being gay like an affliction to be hidden for whatever the reason. You don't have to wave a banner, but if asked, you have two options: "none of your business," which only confirms the question for most; or fess up.

I have found that treating being gay like a nonissue makes it a nonissue. If you make it matter-of-fact, then it becomes just that. But that's a lesson most haven't learned; certainly not Middle America. Normalizing gayness is still a long way off because many gays don't normalize it themselves. They still treat it like a major difference, and so does America. And that's the biggest problem facing the gay community today: normalization. We fear it. We run from it. We do all we can to make sure it doesn't happen. We don't want to assimilate, to become seamless. Whether consciously or unconsciously, most gay people still do quite a bit to point out just how different we are. Pride festivals are proof of that. Exclusively gay bars are proof of that. There are many examples. We want to fit in, but only so much.

And that's fine as well, because certainly we don't want to lose our cultural identity. Being gay is a unique experience, one to be shared and reveled in. But being exclusively gay is dangerous, and being seen as only gay downright calamitous to a public figure.

Is Clay gay? Foley? Who cares, ultimately? We, the people, have the power when it comes to such people. If you don't like the answers they give, one way or the other, don't vote for them, don't buy their records, don't watch their shows. I for one don't watch *Idol,* not because of Clay but because of Ryan. You see, I've worked with him. He is a charming man, and quite fun to be around, actually. And he takes all the gay jokes in stride. But again, he dodges the question. When asked in my presence about being gay, he has always just replied, "Well, everybody thinks I am." He's never said either way, even to me, and we've done 15 TV shows together. I wish him luck, and he's got it right now, but I'd rather be his friend than his fan. As for Clay, until he decides to be honest with the press or himself, I see no need to buy his record. And as for Foley, all I feel is sorry for him—sorry that he would equate being gay to some atrocious crime for which he is being smeared.

We as gays are in a transitional phase. We are on our way to normalizing but haven't reached it yet. People still put the qualifiers first. We're not alone; qualifiers are all around. The black guy down at the corner market. The Asian lady next door. The Arab guy at the 7-Eleven. Americans, people everywhere, use qualifiers. But we need to get to a point where the gay qualifier is no longer a death sentence. Sure, I'm the gay talk-show host, but 10 minutes into the show and suddenly I'm just the guy they disagree with about politics.

How do we get to that point? How do we get the place where Clay, Foley, or anyone else would be fine with the admission? By making it a nonissue. Only we, the gay community, can start that trend. Each day we need to do more to weave ourselves into everyday life for who we are—gayness included but not spotlighted. We must shine as people first, gay people second. We must show by example that beneath the qualifier is someone pretty much the same as everyone else. We must desegregate ourselves, our beliefs, our lifestyle.

The problem with that philosophy is that it takes people like Clay, Foley, me, and you to stand up and answer the question honestly when asked. There's the rub. Until that happens, mainstream America won't see that we are everyone, everywhere. It's a catch-22—one that slowly but surely we can unravel. How? Step up to the plate. It's the hardest thing in the world, but the easiest.

I've Got Mail

Letters, do I get letters...

"Can we please have a break from Charles Karel Bouley II's moralist, self loathing, accusatory diabtribes?"

Always good to wake up to in your in-box. Or how about:

"Quarantining faggots is self loathing. Categorizing all of us as strung out circuit boys who are chasing bugs is self loathing. Deciding that men don't have loving faithful fulfilling relationships anymore, just because you lost your lover and can't find a partner to compare to him is self-loathing. If you get the honor of having your words printed for the masses, you have a responsibility to uplift and not just slander because you hurt."

And then there's always:

"You are a neo-nazi conservative, a right winger's dream who has sold out your very community for the chance to be in the media."

And one of my favorites:

"With all of Karel's faults, it's odd you pick being gay as his first."

It's amazing how many opinions are out there, and amazing how many people attack the messenger and not the message. Most of these letters are in response to my editorials about the gay community. But while I'm not gay enough for them, not supportive enough, not meeting my "responsibility to uplift," go read the Bay Area Broadcasting message boards you'd see that I'm *too* gay for them, that I should be silenced because of my over-the-top queerness and being too support-ive of the gay agenda.

You can't win. Well, maybe *you* can—me, that's another story.

And that's fine, since I signed up for the job. But this lash-ing-out smacks of what is really going on in this country right now, and it's frightening.

As a talk-show host, I took an antiwar position when it came to the bogus Operation Iraqi Freedom. While the rea-son for that position would be another editorial, let's just say I think it was the wrong action at the wrong time, based in half-truths and downright lies that put American soldiers needlessly at risk for oil and for Israel and to fulfill the Project for a New Century's vision drafted seven years ago (do a Google search under that title and you'll see what I mean).

But today, to be antiwar means you are anti-American. It means you are unpatriotic. It means you do not support our troops. Celebrities are being openly Dixie-Chicked over their antiwar stances; Sen. Joseph McCarthy is rolling with glee in his grave as editors get fired and stars get censored (like Tim Robbins and Susan Sarandon, uninvited from the Baseball Hall of Fame's anniversary celebration of *Bull Durham*).

It seems if you speak out against King George II or his regime, you are told to move to Iraq.

The same sentiment seems to go for the gay community. I never wanted to believe it, but by criticizing, questioning, try-ing to talk honestly about the state of being gay, I am a trai-tor, a turncoat, a right-winger, a Nazi. I'm a bitter, self-loathing individual who should be censored or shut up, not published.

I won't explain the reasons I write editorials such as

"Who's SAR-ry Now" or "Time to Turn in My Toaster Oven." They speak for themselves and come from the heart. You see, there's the problem. While most critics seem to think I'm trying to advance some political or social agenda, I'm just writing from the heart, from my experience, from my place of common sense.

But no one really wants to hear that these days. No one in the gay community wants to hear about personal responsibility. No one wants to hear that for all the banner-waving and all the Pride parades, we've still got so long to go. Just look at the current news cycle. Republican senator Santorum from Pennsylvania made strong anti-gay comments and no one cares. He won't have to step down, like Trent Lott did for his flippant remarks about the good old days of racial segregation. In fact, according to 45,908 votes at www.vote.com, Sen. Santorum shouldn't have to be reprimanded or have any negative action taken against him. The White House has not criticized him, as it immediately did Lott—indeed, the official statement was supportive, arguing that Santorum "is an inclusive man." Santorum is another Republican, showing his and his party's true colors, and he will come out of this fine. Why? Because he only pissed off a small portion of the voters. And according to an Associated Press story, and I quote, "Passing judgment on blacks, as in Lott's case, was disastrous because it is now common opinion that discrimination against blacks is wrong. The jury is still out on the national debate about the acceptance of homosexuality."

The jury is still out. It's 2003 and the jury is still out. Am I self-loathing if I say it's pathetic that we have such little organized economic and political clout in this country? Am I a traitor for pointing out that unchecked Santoruptions will probably continue to happen time and time again with little or no repercussions?

Is it self-loathing and hateful to say that during the annual White Party in Palm Springs over Easter weekend, every major news service reported the concern by health officials about gay men giving each other syphilis? *The New York Times* story called it the "weekend known for sex, drugs and dancing"—only confirming what nongays think of us all. And why? Because of some chiseled boys' desire to flaunt their bodies, dance, get high, and have promiscuous sex. Is it hateful to say that making the nation think that 30,000 queers have descended upon the desert to drink, fuck, and spread disease is harmful to the community as a whole and only gives people like Santorum more clout? Am I self-loathing because I say this party has become a public-health issue and may need to go away entirely given the obvious rise in STDs surrounding it *and* the new gay male staph infection epidemic that—like AIDS in its early stages—is now being underreported and downplayed?

I have heard that I am supposed to uplift the community through my radio show and my writing, and not condemn, criticize, be "such a bitter old faggot who should heal or go away." I wonder how many of those critics have demanded the same from the producers of *Queer as Folk* or *Will & Grace,* two shows that only play into the stereotypes of who and what we are and do little to enlighten, uplift, or even entertain.

I am not anti-gay. Much of what I write and say on the air is very pro-gay. Just the fact that I'm on the air is pro-gay. But I guess, as with discussion of the war, I'm supposed to stay superficial and not go beyond the party line. I'm supposed to pay my $50 for the upcoming Long Beach Gay Pride Weekend and go drink and dance and go to the main stage to see Pat Benatar, Chaka Khan, Mary Wilson from the Supremes, members of Starship, and Celia Cruz, not once asking, "Where are the gay entertainers? Why aren't we empowering them by hiring them?" Where's Ashley MacIsaac, who is out promoting a new album? Where's Boy? Where's George Michael? Hell, I'd settle for Paul Lekakis or even RuPaul. But I shouldn't ask that question. I shouldn't wonder why the cover of my hometown Gay Pride program doesn't have one gay person on it.

I should shut up and continue to watch gay men screw themselves into extinction while busy talking about empowering ourselves in dedicated, long-term couples. But speaking as someone who was half of one long-term couple, and speaking for those of you who are now coupled, you know that if you are a dedicated, long-term couple, the only way to survive as such is basically to drop out of the gay community and live your life at Home Depot, potlucks, movies, plays, and other outlets, like your married heterosexual counterparts. Why? Because our community doesn't provide entertainment options for married couples. In fact, most of our public outlets for socializing are counterproductive to coupling all together. But again, I digress back to self-loathing. Right?

This is how I write: I hold a mirror up to myself and examine all parts of who I am, my gayness included. And then I write about the reflection, the entire thing, not just parts. I write positive columns, like "My Big Gay Moments," reveling in the fact that it's great to be a gay male. I constantly talk on the air about how wonderful it is to be open, to be out, to be yourself—and how we must allow everyone the same right.

But that is forgotten.

What's remembered is that I dare to say the things I find in my heart that people don't want to hear, and because of it I'm broken, I need to be fixed.

One e-mailer said, "Do us a favor and don't write until you heal some of the bitterness inside of you." But maybe it's not me but the community that needs to heal. It's been on the defensive so long, it can't even open a dialogue about what is right and what is wrong. Everything's fine, we all behave wonderfully, and we're moving quickly to equal rights in all the States.

Say it with me, one more time: poppycock.

There's only one thing worse than being in the closet, and that's having your head in the sand. (For one thing, it gets in the hair and never comes out. But I digress.)

I love what I see when I look around me. I love it enough to want it to be better, to want it to reach its full potential. I cry when I realize we're still powerless against people like Santorum, and I rejoice when something wonderful happens for the community like AB 25 in California. I revel in it all, not just part of it. And we all should do the same. Love the great stuff, talk about the bad. Calling someone a sellout because they show unflattering parts is just what Middle America does in its inflated post–9/11 idea of patriotic fervor. What does that get? The USA Patriot Act, which removes more civil rights in one swoop than anything since the Constitution was ratified. Middle America sat by and let that happen. Are we gays and lesbians going to continue to sit by and basically self-destruct because we're afraid to look at ourselves from all sides, including those that are the least flattering, the sides that need some help? I hope not, because we have so much to teach the world about love, understanding, kindness, joy—and, of course, fashion.

The Little Pink Schoolhouse

High school was tough. I remember it vividly. I went to an inner-city school known as much for school violence as for its football team. It was a true melting pot: white, black, Hispanic, Samoan, Asian—you name it, we had it. And yes, gay. I dated a boy in high school and everyone knew I was gay; I couldn't hide it. It brought me some trouble and taught me a lot about the real world and how it wouldn't necessarily welcome me with open arms. It taught me how to get out of potentially dangerous situations using wit and sometimes my feet to flee. It taught me about life outside the confines of the campus.

So it is with great trepidation that I heard the news last month that New York is starting the nation's first full-scale school for gay, lesbian, bisexual, transgendered, and—I hate this part—questioning youth. We already have too many letters in our moniker and don't need to add a *q*, but that's another essay.

In any event, the powers that be all think it's a grand and glorious idea to expand the nonprofit Hetrick-Martin Institute's 20-year-old alternative high school program from its existing two-room existence into a full-on public high school for GLBT (and, um, Q) students, keeping the same name, Harvey Milk High School.

"I think everybody feels that it's a good idea because some of the kids who are gays and lesbians have been constantly harassed and beaten in other schools," Mayor Michael Bloomberg said to ABC News in a briefing on July 28. "It let's them get an education without having to worry. It solves a discipline problem."

Well, maybe the honorable mayor thinks that "everybody feels it's a good idea," but I do not.

First, part of a good education for gay youth is to learn how to deal with being constantly harassed and beaten. I know that sounds harsh, but so is real life. Isolating youth, protecting them from the dangers of a world that doesn't always accept them, doesn't always treat them right, is the wrong thing to do. It leads to more deaths like those of Matthew Shepard and Gwen Araujo.

Using the justification that "this will solve a discipline problem" is by far the worst cop-out I've heard yet. It's like saying, "Well, we can't seem to make these kids any more tolerant, we can't seem to stop them from beating these gay kids, so we'd better remove the gay kids for their own good." Say it with me: poppycock.

How on Earth can we ever expect young students to grow up and be more tolerant, more apt to support gay legislation, more apt to not beat a gay person to death if we can't even stop them from doing it in school? If we just throw in the towel and say, "Oh, it's too dangerous for the kids here, we'd better move them," as opposed to removing the danger right where they are?

It's defeatist. It's wrong. It dashes any hope we might have or raising a more tolerant, peaceful generation of children.

Isolationism is not the way to treat gay youth. Removing them from social situations that may be harmful isn't the answer. The answer is to teach them how to better integrate with their peers and discipline or, if necessary, remove the troublemakers. Punish the child who refuses to learn tolerance.

How about making a special school for the intolerant, instead of vice versa? How about isolating all of those who would hurt or oppress anyone who is different because of sexuality, skin color, etc.? Oh, I forgot, we have those special programs already—it's called going to high school in the Bible Belt.

I have watched many brave youth across the country fight their schools for the right to have gay-straight alliances—extracurricular student groups to promote mutual respect, tolerance clubs; call them what you will. They fought within the system to bring understanding into the system. They often had to fight their parents and the parents on the school board more than the other students themselves. Let's remember: Intolerant children usually come from intolerant parents. And how are we going to protect our youth from those adults, who are the real source of their woes and will remain so throughout their lives? Move them right from the gay high school in to gay college (Gertrude and Alice University?) and then a cute condo in West Hollywood, the Castro, or Greenwich Village? Nonsense.

While many see the expansion of Harvey Milk High as a brave step forward, I see it as a monstrous step backwards. If a private institute like Hetrick-Martin wants to start a school that caters to gay youth, and parents wish to put their children into that program, fine. It's their choice—as are religious schools, single-sex boarding schools, and so on. But when it comes to public schools removing the "gay element," that sends a dangerous message that the brutes have won. It sends a message that different people belong in different, private places. It sends a message to gay youth that they need protecting, coddling; special needs.

Gay youth are not special needs children, like those with disabilities or discipline problems. They don't need to ride the short yellow bus to school or have special P.E. And they certainly don't need their own school. What they need is for administrators to actually do their jobs and not be afraid to make those who would judge or oppress gay kids feel like the outcasts, instead of the gay students. They need the school board to recognize that a class in tolerance and equality is just as important in the grand scheme of things as a course in algebra or wood shop—perhaps even more crucial in today's world.

Yes, change in the public school system is needed. We need to realize that teaching social skills and how to interact with each other in harmony is just as important as the actual academics.

Schools don't work as they are now—as evidenced by test scores, attendance, and their current state of decay in many districts. We have it backwards. We make classrooms and schools smaller when children are younger, and then have massive high schools when they're older, some with 2,000 or more students.

Great, let's put 2,000 kids together, hormones raging, and see what happens. Ridiculous. High schools should be much smaller, with smaller classes and more individualized attention. We're making adults here, not robots. Have larger K-9 schools, and smaller Grade 9 and above, so troublemakers can be more easily identified. It may stop some gay children from being hurt, and it may stop tragedies like Columbine from happening again.

But no. Instead we do what we always do: We solve a problem without thinking what it does to our cultural collective. Isolating gay students is not something we should pat ourselves on the back for—it means we failed, the public school system failed, and our gay leaders believe we have to retreat to the barricaded solace of 2 Astor Place in the East Village. And if I were a parent of a nongay student in New York City, I'd be a bit upset that a $3.2 million renovation is going on to create this school while many others in the inner city don't have computers or even adequate lunch programs.

No, this fall's opening of Harvey Milk High will not be a

proud day for me. It is yet another day that I will see us moving backwards, not forwards. It is a day I see us sending a dangerous message to all youth: "If you don't like someone, beat them, and sooner or later they'll leave, either by choice or fear."

Well, I and many of my generation made it through school just fine. Oh, yes, I was beaten a few times, shoved in a locker, called names. But so was Bill Gates, and now he owns the universe. Character is built in high school. Personalities are forged. We can't protect everyone from the evils of the world, and when we try, people die of naïvété.

I would much rather see programs for gay youth incorporated in to current school programs, as has been done, successfully, around the country. We don't need our own school, our own city, our own planet. In the immortal words of Tracy Turnblad, "Segregation never, Integration now!"

Defending Marriage

So here I sit, having just survived Marriage Protection Week. It seems conservative Christians, including those in the White House, decided that October 12-18, 2003, should be a week set aside to protect marriage. A presidential proclamation was issued. This is serious stuff. Marriage must be in a terrible state.

Even cast in its best light, this is sheer homophobia. At a time when more and more states are wrestling with the legalities or illegalities of recognizing the unions of same-sex couples, right-wingers are fearful that some state (can you say "Massachusetts"?) might actually allow gays to marry their partners. This, they say, would destroy marriage. So it must be protected.

And no, President Bush, your Marriage Protection Week is not about lowering divorce rates, or better access to couples counseling, or preventing domestic violence, or ensuring a nurturing environment for children. It's about hating gay people. This, for example, is from MarriageProtectionWeek.com:

> The sacred institution of marriage is under attack. There are those who want to redefine marriage to include two men, or two women, or a group of any size or mix of sexes: One man and four women, one woman and two

men, etc. If they fail to secure legal protection classifying these arrangements as 'marriage,' they want to include all these mixtures under the definition of 'civil union,' giving them identical standing with the marriage of one man and one woman. They have gained the support of the national media and many politicians. Their efforts are intended to force, by law, 97% of Americans to bow down to the desires of the approximately 3% who are homosexuals. To call attention to this most critical issue...you, your church or group is encouraged to help protect the sacred institution of marriage.

Anyone who says this is anything but White House-endorsed gay bashing is lying.

There is a valid argument that we need a movement to protect marriage. But marriage doesn't need protection from people who have never been allowed to participate. Nay, it needs protection from those who have allowed it to become the disposable, litigious, carefree institution that it is now.

Before we get to the "defense of marriage" issue, let's look at what everyone wants to defend. Marriage, first and foremost, is a legal agreement about property and property rights. It has had many forms. It wasn't always referred to as *marriage*, a word that came to English from the 14th-century French *marier*.

Let's look even further back: The principal property that marriage was developed to deal with—a property that is still the core right of marriage in many cultures across the globe—is the woman. In this most traditional, most historically accurate form of marriage, the woman is considered a possession: first of her father, then of her lawful husband. She has little voice in where she lives; what her husband does; whether, or how many children they have; or her own duties and chores in the arrangement. She is expected to devote herself to her husband and her family. (Think this is from long, long ago?

It's only been since the emergence of feminism that "love, honor, and obey" in the woman's vows in most Christian ceremonies was reduced to two out of three of those.) Historically, wives were often awarded to men for great victories or feats of strength and bravery. Sometimes they were—and still are—simply sold outright.

As time went by, the property of the wife was joined by all kinds of other property rights that were settled by marriage: joining lands controlled by multiple families; allotting a portion of one family's wealth to the heir of another family with the proviso that Junior marries Missy; creating heirs so that all the lands and wealth could be passed along and kept all in the family. And so on.

According to these millennia-old traditions, marriage is a contract that has nothing to do with faith, religion, God, or the like. It has everything to do with real estate, wealth, lines of succession, and business and political negotiations. The notion of marriage as a Christian sacrament and not just a contract can be traced back to Saint Paul, who in his letter to the Ephesians compared the relationship of husband and wife to that of Christ and the church. The troubadours in the 12th century were the first cultural force to encourage the idea that love—love in the way we think of it now—should be the primary impulse for two people to commit to one another.

In the 1500s there were so many marriages taking place without ceremony or witnesses that the Council of Trent, a Catholic body to counter the Protestant Reformation, decreed in 1563 that marriages should be celebrated in the presence of a priest and two witnesses. Marriage, by this time, was a way to prevent men and women from sins, a union for companionship and for procreation. Love wasn't necessarily invited.

The Puritans referred to marriage as "the highest and most blessed of relationships." The idealization of the monogamous marriages rose to its peak during the Victorian period, thanks in part to a lot of puritanical Christians of all denominations. Sex, at that time, was embarrassing and improper unless there was that quiet understanding that married couples enjoyed doing the nasty as a duty to God.

So marriage started out about property and then became about love—to some degree. Even today, it's still about property, and yes, women are still seen as such, even in these United States. Until fairly recently, married women still needed their husband's signature to obtain a credit card or a mortgage; single women were much less likely than single men to enjoy those same privileges. In 1970s Texas a woman couldn't have a tubal ligation without her husband's consent unless a preset goal was reached: a certain age, a certain number of children, etc.

These days marriage has evolved, and not for the better. While the White House and right-wing Christians scream that two people who actually *want* to enter into this sacrament could destroy it, they ignore the number one killer of marriages: divorce. If protecting marriage is what they're after, leave gays and lesbians alone and go after divorce. It is a blight on marriage, on this country, and on our economy.

According to the U.S. National Center for Health Statistics, for every two marriages that occurred in the 1990s there was one divorce. An estimated 40% of the U.S. women born in the 1970s will divorce. In Missouri alone, 22,511 children had parents who divorced in 2000. Nationally, divorce costs the U.S. taxpayers billions of dollars per year in deadbeat dads, support for abused women and children, welfare support, and so on. Divorce affects the psyche of children in the marriage. Murders have been committed in messy divorces. Divorce is a billion-dollar industry for lawyers and financial advisers and such.

Yes, the ease with which married couples can get a divorce is the real scourge. If these right-wing groups and our president were really interested in saving and protecting marriage, they would outlaw divorce except in extreme cases. Instead of excluding people from getting into the institution, they need to make it harder for those in it to get out.

Why don't they launch campaigns against those who defame marriage? Why not campaign against television networks that air shows like *Joe Millionaire* and *The Bachelor* and *Who Wants to Marry a Multimillionaire?* and *Temptation Island?* Why elect anyone who has had a divorce? How about Newt Gingrich? Where was their outrage when he was carrying on an affair before he was divorced? How about impeaching any president for extramarital affairs because they are setting such a bad example of the sanctity of marriage? Where's the proclamation for that? How many U.S. senators are on their second or third wives? Henry VIII started an entirely new church because the pope wouldn't sanction his divorce and new marriage. Where's that kind of commitment now?

The truth is that neither the president nor his right-wing allies are interested at all in protecting marriage. They are interested in being bigoted homophobes who want to deface the U.S. Constitution with the first-ever amendment that would deny a group of people the same rights that others have, based solely on a partner's sex. They fear because they know that one day sane courts will not allow this inequality to continue because it is, at base, unconstitutional. So they launch these campaigns. But they should at least have the decency to call Marriage Protection Week what it was: Sanction Attacks on Gays and Lesbians Week.

It's so amusing to me, because while the anti-gay forces scream about "protecting marriage" from us evil homos, gays and lesbians are actually better role models about marriage then those who can actually get married. You see, I was with my partner, Andrew, for almost 12 years before his death. We didn't stay together because of the fear of the litigation involved in a divorce. We didn't stay together to protect some facade of what married life should be. We didn't stay together because some piece of paper or ceremony made us feel obligated. We didn't stay together for the kids. We stayed together because we loved each other, because we wanted to build something beautiful together. Because we *were* married, in spirit and soul.

Gays and lesbians face so much discrimination that our relationships are looked upon as second-class. I say that any gay man or lesbian who is able to stay in a "married" relationship deserves awards and accolades, not exclusion. Because they beat the odds.

The gay community doesn't foster relationships; never has. Most activities are for singles. Once gays get "married" they tend to bond more with their married heterosexual counterparts. But these couples survive the odds, and most flourish. They stay together because of connection, of love. And they should be entitled to the same property rights, rights of succession, probate, inheritance, etc., that any straight guy can earn by getting drunk, flying to Vegas, and marrying a Vietnamese hooker so she can stay in the country. We deserve the same benefits Liz Taylor got with her—what is it now?—eight husbands? Nine? Or J. Lo with her two, or the corporate executive who divorces his aging wife and marries his secretary, or Anna Nicole Smith.

Yes, marriage needs protection. There's a lot of work to be done to turn it back into a valid, indisposable, and even sacred institution. But again, bigots are shortsighted. They're fighting the right war but with the wrong enemy. They're at the wrong border, fighting the wrong front. They could have powerful allies in the gay community—even more people willing to fight with them to make marriage matter. Instead, they choose to call our unions evil.

Well, there have been many evil marriages. Arranged marriages, marriages where women die from abuse, or where children get tied to bedposts for five years of their lives covered in feces. Marriages where husbands have waged war and killed thousands to gain the hand of a lady so they could expand their empires. Yes, there have been many dangerous, evil, horrendous marriages. And not *one* of them has been between two members of the same sex. Perhaps they should think about that when they are defending their institution.

World AIDS Day:
Where's the Parade?

It's December 1, 2003. To most people it's just Monday. But to many it's World AIDS Day. Of course, none of my gay friends knew about it. Maybe they're just uniformed. Few of my listeners knew about it, and when I told them, they all wondered what they were supposed to *do* for World AIDS Day.

In 1988, World AIDS Day (or WAD, a funny acronym if ever I heard one) was conceived and adopted unanimously by 140 countries meeting at the World Summit of Ministers of Health on AIDS in London. The day, according to their Web site, was envisioned as an opportunity for governments, national AIDS programs, and nongovernmental and local organizations as well as individuals to demonstrate both the importance they attached to the fight against AIDS and their solidarity in this effort. Well, like most do-gooder political plans, this one has fallen flat.

First and foremost, the news on World AIDS Day is not good. In fact, most figures are worse than ever. Globally, AIDS claimed three million people last year. That's about 8,000 per day. About 14,000 new cases of HIV infection occur every day around the world. Ninety-five percent of all AIDS cases occur in the world's poorest countries, and in many at least one in five or one in four adults are HIV-positive.

In America, African-American women make up the fastest-growing number of new AIDS cases, and in another study, young gay men under 25 and Latinos are topping the new infections list in the U.S. more than ever. Around the globe, 42 million people are now living with AIDS. In the U.S. alone 200,000 are suspected to be infected without their knowing it. And 46% of new AIDS infections in the U.S. were reported in our Southern states.

So, on the 18th observance of WAD, things are worse than ever. The UN is launching a campaign to get drugs to three million people who cannot afford them, mostly in Third World nations and sub-Sahara Africa. And there are other ambitious plans. Even the Pope has prayed for people with AIDS. He should—his church helped many contract the disease through their clandestine and archaic approach to contraception in other nations.

So, why are we here, in a ship that appears to be sinking faster than rising as public interest in AIDS wanes and gay men in the U.S. still don't seem to have a clue? Well, as someone who lived with an HIV-positive man for 11-plus years, as someone who has been out and gay forever and has been a primary care giver for many years, I have a few opinions about it.

First, religion still is one of the main reasons AIDS has spread outside of the United States, and in it (especially in the South). The stigma surrounding AIDS, sex, and homosexuality make religion a giant obstacle in the road to fighting AIDS. People are afraid to disclose their status, talk about their illness, get treatment—all because of their religious beliefs. Churches weren't quick to alter their perspective on contraceptives, safe sex, and the dissemination of information about AIDS, and now people, religious people, are paying the price. And in other countries, other theocracies like our own, it's even worse. Imagine having HIV in a Muslim nation, a Communist nation, war-torn nations like Vietnam...it's easy to see why there's such a problem.

Then comes the biggest problem: apathy. As my listeners attested last night, AIDS has been around for more than 20 years and people are tired of it from the standpoint that many heterosexuals feel it's preventable, so how long do we continue in the U.S. to feel compassion for so many who are simply ignorant and get the disease? Because that's why people get it in 2003 for the most part: ignorance. We're not talking blood transfusions here; we're talking gay men and intravenous drug users in the U.S. People are sick of hearing about how more and more gay men are getting HIV when we know how to prevent contracting the virus.

So who failed here? Did the word not get out enough? Why are we still at this point?

Well, we all failed.

AIDS organizations failed in so many ways, I could write 100 editorials about them. From their own politics tying their hands, to the pressure from Washington to do things the Bush way, which is to preach abstinence only. AIDS organizations are not reaching mainstream gay or straight communities, as statistics will attest. And while many do lots of good, the politics of it all has kept them from being truly effective. Again, that statement is backed up by the numbers.

The U.S. government continues to fail its own people—and people across the world—by constantly changing policies, shifting tone, and using money as a bargaining tool to promote their own social agenda.

We gay men have failed, by becoming complacent and being short-sighted. I maintain that any gay man that contracts HIV in this day and age deserves it because ignorance is no excuse given the extensive outreach to our community for more than 20 years. We seem not to want to shoulder our responsibility in the spread of this disease. Live for the moment. Well, moments are running out for so many.

And the entire AIDS system has failed. The billion-dollar-a-year business that is AIDS has yet to find an effective way to reach those who need to be reached. World AIDS Day? Please. Many don't know if they should organize a parade, cry over the quilt, or go hug someone with HIV. No one I've spoken to really knows what to do on World AIDS Day.

And what about WAD? Do we have world hepatitis day? World Herpes Day? How did this virus get its own holiday? I mean, if you look at the numbers, as bad as they are, they are tiny. Out of more than six billion people in the world, only 42 million are HIV-positive. When you put it in that perspective, you see that while AIDS is devastating the planet (as virus and germs were meant to do—an early form of population control) it's not wiping it out. It's wiping out poor people, ignorant people, complacent people, oppressed people, irresponsible people, innocent people, and saints alike. It's doing what a virus does, getting into the body and killing based on blood, not on anything else. The virus doesn't care, but it's found a home in poverty and irresponsibility.

So, what do we do? Well, I don't think a holiday is the answer. What is? I honestly don't know. For once I'm perplexed. You see, how do we make every person responsible for their own actions? How do we educate an entire globe when there are so many social, religious, and political obstacles to that honest education? How do we do what should have been done 20 years ago and move this from a social disease to a medical one? Well, simply put: We don't. We can't.

But what we can do is control our own world. Start there. Make sure you are safe, and that everyone you know hears the safety-first speech repeatedly. Make it chic to use condoms. Make casual sex a rarity, not the norm. Donate carefully to organizations, checking them out first to make sure the actually do something for people with AIDS. Support frank discussions in schools, put pressure on school boards to continue teaching real-world sex education, not the Bush plan, but the real one. And older gays, those of us over 40—take the time to educate our own, our youth, who are the ones starting the third wave of this pandemic. Seldom do older gays become mentors, tutors...they're just looked upon as trolls and skimmed over. Well, start grass roots movements in your community to make sure the real message about gay sex gets out there. Make sure young and old gays around you know that it's their choice whether or not to deal with the virus. They can stay clear of it easily, or they can let Absolut or ecstasy take them down a path that will lead to much heartbreak, even death. In other words, we really need to do a better job of policing our own.

Why? Because there should be a ZERO infection rate among gay men. We should lead the way in showing the world how to deal with this disease, since we've been dealing with it for more than two decades. Instead of the press releases on WAD stating how we have more infections than ever, they should be saying gay men are leading the way to zero transmission. Of course, that would require a change in thinking and lifestyle, and we know how likely that is. But we can hope.

And maybe that's what today is supposed to be about. Hope. I have hope for less lethal treatments. For a cure. For a vaccine. I have hope for gay men finally realizing that a bare dick or cum isn't worth the cost. I have hope that governments will stop skimping and start demanding that these multi-billion-dollar drug companies heal those within their power. I have hope that World AIDS Day won't be needed in 10 years.

Thank You, Mr. President

Politicians are morons, at least the ones in true positions of power. Somehow, someplace, they learned that confrontation, divisiveness, and moral outrage send voters to the polls, so now that is all they concentrate on. Gone are real issues that face the nation, such as our health care system, failed foreign policies, and teetering economy. Welcome back abortion and same-sex marriage.

The politicians—president, candidates, and pundits—put same-sex marriage on the agenda for 2004, a time America clearly shows through polls that it doesn't care. But no, this year, we're going to care, like it or not. And that sucks because it means battle lines are drawn and now there's no compromise.

You see, I wasn't a big fan of gay marriage before all of this. I—and my late husband, Andrew—felt it was an unwinnable battle politically and that the state of marriage wasn't much to boast about. So on our radio show we supported domestic partnerships on a federal level with all—not some, but *all*—the benefits of marriage, open to same-sex couples as well as mixed-sex couples, period. Federally rec-

ognized domestic partnerships: leave the word *marriage* totally out of it. What you do with your church is your business.
Let's make things equal at city hall.

Later, when Andrew died of what I allege to be malpractice, I fell victim to our inability to get married. After 11-plus
years together I remained, under the law, his friend. We had
filed a domestic partnership agreement, and now there
appears to be recourse thanks to AB 25, the California bill
signed by now-former governor Gray Davis that strengthens
the state's DP law. But the legal hoopla—and the lawyers, and
the hearings, and the insults—that I've had to endure are
amazing when a simple "I do" would have solved it all.

Yet I didn't get angry and say, "If we could have been married..." What I said was, "If only there were federal domestic
partnership..."

Now I can't say that anymore. I have to support same-sex
marriage, because the ongoing presidential attack on gay
marriage isn't about marriage at all. It can't be. Letting people who want to enter in to a loving, binding institution willingly could only help that institution, not hurt it. Ending no-
fault divorce could help it, for example. No, this is about
national gay bashing. This is about a federal mandate against
the citizenship status of gays and lesbians. It's plain, clear-cut,
religiously motivated homophobia that cannot be tolerated.

A president should be impeached for suggesting that "the
people" take a course to amend a document set up to protect
civil rights into something that denies the very equal protection promised in its pages. And to do it based on religious values is exactly why the framers wanted to separate church and
state. This is the founding fathers' worst nightmare happening: creating a new breed of second-class citizens (assuming
their spirits have since thought better about that whole slavery thing). They would be the first to call for impeachment.

Even if the president's anti-gay sentiments reflected the
mood of the people, it wouldn't be right and it wouldn't fit

with the spirit of the constitution. People must be led by law, according to our government, and those laws are based on certain truths, and we hold these truths to be self evident, that all men were created equal.

What part of "all" don't the zealots understand? In how many parts of our Constitution and Declaration of Independence would they like to delete the word *equal*? It seems that now that the courts are starting to see that gays and lesbians are part of that "all" and those "equals," the zealots are afraid.

So now an all-out social war has been declared. It's a battle over an issue that didn't have to go this way, that didn't have to be so big, and it will divide so many at a time when unity is needed. And it's making people like me choose sides. There was a compromise in sight, one that could have been done state by state until most states had realized how stupid this all is and simply legalized marriage or domestic partnerships, and then there would have been a national judicial consensus. Of course, that's what the zealots fear: rational people forced to make a rational decision based on the principles on which this nation was established. Like it or not, "all" means "all"—not "some" or just the ones you approve of.

Because there's no compromise available anymore, I must be a soldier in a battle that didn't need to be fought this way. And I have to be on a side that I was not totally committed to. All Americans will find themselves in the same place, not because any of them really and truly want to be there or give a rat's ass about who marries whom, but because the media and the power players want to win, so they want to divide and conquer. The losers the gay and lesbian citizens of this country who will have to hear daily about how they are welcomed but just don't fully belong, how they're God's children but immoral and how we should all treat them with compassion but not with equality.

Nobody wins in this battle. Those who would rather the

issue not be an issue now have to face it, and those who have always wanted the issue to be at the forefront may not be ready for the battle or the outcome. But let's be clear on the issue: It's not same-sex marriage, it's gays and lesbians—period. It's our existence, our very ability to live and work in this country without harm, discrimination, or intrusion. It's about a national no stamp being placed on the forehead of every gay and lesbian American citizen. And America should be careful: Those stamps will appear on their children, parents, sons, daughters, wives, husbands, cousins, friends, families—their world.

But I hope we, the gay and lesbian community, fight this fight with dignity. Common sense, decency, and the Constitution are on our side at the moment. Perhaps this all happened around the celebration of Martin Luther King Jr.'s birthday for a reason: maybe to remind us that we must be better than those who lead the war on the other side. We must remain visible, nonviolent, and unified. So far, we're not so hot on two out of three of those. But we are remarkable as a community, and I am reminded of that by my circle of friends. We are great people as a whole. Now some of us must step beyond our comfort zones of outness and get involved in this battle.

How? Education on the issue. First, if an amendment is being thrown about, how about telling everyone what that process is? Do you know? If not, go directly to www.uscon-stitution.net and learn about the amendment process. In short, it's like this: Short of having a constitutional convention declared by two thirds of the states, an amendment has to pass both houses of Congress by a two-thirds majority, then it had to be approved again by three quarters of the state legislatures (or 38 states—a smaller number than have already passed state laws outlawing recognition of same-sex marriage). The president, you may note, has no role in any of this: He can't introduce an amendment, and he can't veto one if it's passed.

The amendment process is complex, costly, and time-consuming. Time is an important factor: After Congress passes an amendment, it usually gives the states a fixed number of years to ratify an amendment before it expires without becoming part of the Constitution. That's what happened to the Equal Rights Amendment, which would have codified (to use the president's favorite word) a prohibition against sex discrimination. Congress passed it, but seven years passed and fewer than 38 states had ratified it. Congress extended the deadline, but the future looks bleak.

It's all utterly ridiculous, when you actually look at the issue: Does the United States of America have the collective right to tell a large percentage of its tax base that they don't have the same equal rights to "life, liberty, and the pursuit of happiness" promised in our Declaration of Independence? To limit their rights in the form of an amendment to the very document that protects them? Any rational true American, be they homophobe or not, if thinking through they eyes of the framers, would say no, it doesn't have that right, and in fact has no right at all to stop them from enjoying all the benefits of other citizens—including the right to marry.

But the battle to get rational thinkers to think and act rationally will be a highly emotional and irrational one. And it's one that didn't have to happen.

Thank you, Mr. President, for dividing a nation even more. Thank you, Mr. President, for making me now choose a side. Thank you, Mr. President, for once again proving a lot of power with little sensibility is a dangerous, dangerous thing.

Wolves in Sheep's Clothing
Will Still Tear You Apart

I love waking up angry. Well, actually, I don't, but sometimes you don't get a choice. Like today, Feb. 24, 2004.
Today the Republican president of the United States held a
press conference to support a Constitutional amendment banning same-sex marriage.

It wasn't his stance that angered me. Well, it was, but I've
known his stance for some time. It was the timing and the spirit
in which it was done. First of all, his holding a press conference
to come out in favor of an amendment not yet introduced was
interesting. As he spoke, a Republican from Colorado was flying
to Washington to introduce a 51-word amendment. So what he
was saying wasn't that he supported an existing amendment but
that he wanted one introduced *now*. His Republican sycophants
were ready to respond in kind.

Why did he need them? Because he can't introduce an
amendment; it's not in his power.

So today 30-plus million Americans were told their unions
were so horrible that the very document that sets out to pro-

tect them must be altered. Of course, he won't get the two-thirds votes needed as the first steps to ratify said amendment in both houses of Congress. But that doesn't matter. He'll get what he wants in an election year, a weapon of mass distraction. The nation now will talk about this. I bet if you ask a parent of a soldier killed in Iraq, they'd say they *don't* want to talk about this. But when have Republicans really cared about the people they govern? If you're not white, wealthy, and Christian by their definition, then forget it.

As I sit here hearing the debates begin, I start to reminisce. I remember vividly a lunch I had almost two years ago. It was at Hamburger Mary's in Long Beach, Calif., where I live. I was there to meet Young Jason, a.k.a Y.J. We often met for lunch in those days. This day was different, however. Today Y.J. brought a huge stack of papers, computer printouts from various Web sites, and piled them in front of me like letters to Santa piled in front of the judge in *Miracle on 34th Street* (the original, black-and-white version).

The reason for this information deluge was to prove to me once and for all that President George W. Bush and his administration had in fact done good things for gays and lesbians and were progressive, inclusive, and compassionately conservative. The day before, via instant messaging, we had had a vicious debate in which I maintained the Administration was totally inept in regard to gays and lesbians and that anyone who voted for Bush had betrayed us. Y.J. was here to prove me wrong.

Now it's almost two years later, after the State of the Union address and today's press conference spewing Bush's affirmations of his firm conviction that gays and lesbians don't deserve equal rights, Y.J. expressed via another IM regret for ever voting for this guy. I got to say a really wonderful "I told you so" and remind him of that epic lunch. He told me I still deserved that paper deluge because I had been mean. I said amending the constitution to take rights away from one group of Americans was ultimately meaner.

Cut to last week. I went out, which is a rare event for me these days. After my mother lost her battle with chronic obstructive pulmonary disorder (the nation's fourth biggest killer, but that's another story) on December 29, I was pretty glad to be anyplace. A very handsome young man called Moose came over to say hello. He had auditioned for a role in *Second Story* (a play and movie I'm self-producing) and was actually perfect for it. Since my mother went into a nursing home July 29, during preproduction, I put the movie on hold. I assumed he was coming up to offer his condolences and ask about the movie, which he was, but he also wanted to talk politics. This interested me, since he's only 21.

Suddenly he said the words "as a Republican..."

Well, I listened to his banter until he said that if the president softens his stance on marriage, he's voting for him. And even if he doesn't change his position on marriage equality, his other policies are outstanding and on the right track. (I wonder which track he felt POTUS was on this morning.)

I stopped, like in the film *Requiem for a Dream*—that "everyone around you goes at lightning speed and you are standing still" kind of stopped. And then I burst in to a tirade only a seasoned, impassioned radio talk-show host could do in the middle of a bar.

Afterward, I was so angry. I have always wondered how any self-respecting gay person could identify as a Republican. I've always thought it was like a black person joining the KKK. Truly, I have. I know that's bigoted and wrong of me, but it's how I feel. The Republican Party has never helped gays and lesbians to any great degree and has sometimes wanted to round us up and put us on a range in Montana. Reagan let a generation die of AIDS by his inaction and by ignoring the agony of his nation, allegedly because the lifestyle of those afflicted conflicted with his religious beliefs. I've watched Republican candidates blatantly hand back money from Log Cabiners. And

I've always wondered why any gay person would want to be a Republican. And today, after this, why isn't every Log Cabin club turning in its charter?

When I ask gay Republicans why they don't give it up, I get the same response: They're going to change the party from the inside out, to make a difference inside the tent instead of in another camp, and because of a belief in the Republican ideology. Well, I have issue with all of that. I think it's something they tell themselves so they can sleep at night. I hope tonight they need Ambien.

First and foremost is the ideology. What is the Republican ideology? I grew up thinking, hearing, reading that Republicans were for fiscal responsibility, less government, that they were pro-business and somewhat conservative, and that Democrats were blatant tax-and-spenders, wanted huge government-socialism, really wanted to create a very antibusiness climate due to regulations, and were tree-hugging, save-the-whales liberals. I think most people born in the 1960s had that view of the parties, and that's why I think gay men and women believe they can still be Republican. But that platform is long gone. Sometime between Sonny and Cher's divorce and Krystle and Alexis's padded-shoulder tussles it all went away. And gays and lesbians need to realize exactly what alliances they're making politically right now, at a time of declared social civil war against them.

Republicans are not for less government, as they call for amending the Constitution to institutionalize bigotry in the very document on which our democracy is founded. According to an ABCNews.com story by John Stossel about media myths, no Republican administration has cut the size of government for over 75 years, and since George W. Bush became president government spending has risen nearly 25%. The money isn't just for the war on terror. The Office of Management and Budget reports that spending is up 12% at the Environmental Protection Agency, 14% at the Agriculture

Department, 30% at the Department of the Interior, 64% at the Department of Labor, and 70% at the Department of Education. And let's not forget the entirely new branch of the government, the Department of Homeland Security, created under a Republican regime, and how much that cost taxpayers. What did we get for that so far, for that new governmental department? Suggestions of duct tape and plastic. Money well spent, I'm sure.

As for fiscal responsibility, George W. Bush is on a spending spree and has created, according to a January 27, 2004 report on CNN, an almost $2 trillion—with a *t*—deficit for the grandchildren of present day Americans to pay off. While Reagan was creating financial disasters with trickle-down economics, the wealthiest 1% of the nation got better tax breaks while the working class bore the brunt.

As for being "conservative," the Republican Party has let strong right-wing Christian influences dominate it and its platform for 16 years or more now, whether more moderate Republicans like it or not. The mouthpieces for the party are Christian zealots—all of them, including the president—and the rest of the party hasn't policed them or found muzzles big enough to silence them. Republicans tried to corner the market on "family values" and "true American" tradition and in doing so made those values and traditions good ol' right-wing Christian values, beliefs that condemn homosexuality unconditionally. It is now part of their platform, their agenda, to make sure America follows the far right and to have us all help finance it, with faith-based initiatives and school voucher programs.

And as for less government, Republicans now habitually create new policy, legislation, government, regulations, not to rein in corporations that are raping the taxpayers for billions in bailouts (can you say Enron?) but to limit the rights of American citizens at the grassroots levels, now including the Constitution. Enter the debate on abortion, gay marriage, "runaway litigation," and a host of other social issues, things the Right thinks are wrong, so what's left?

The Republican Party once stood for states' rights and still touts them. That is a broken board in their platform as well. The attorney general's office under John Ashcroft (who has prayer meetings in the a.m. and won't dance) has gone after states that have voted to legalize medical marijuana and assisted suicide, two things the Right won't have. They will say when you die, not you, and their drug buddies want to keep you away from a natural herb that can actually help your suffering if you have AIDS, cancer, or other illnesses so they can sell you other, more toxic substances, far more addictive, lethal, and expensive than pot. So the feds say no to the states and go after them in federal court while making raids on poor people in line buying pot so they don't puke.

States' rights? Please. The people spoke, but it was something Washington and the Right didn't want to hear, so their voices and votes didn't matter.

And as for family values, what kind of father supports a law that would bar his daughter, a lesbian, from enjoying the same benefits he enjoys in his marriage? The vice president of the United States, Republican Dick Cheney.

So much for the Republican platform. I won't even address the "no child left behind" (never funded) or "compassionate conservative" mantras, as drug addicts sit in jail, Martha Stewart goes on trial, and we make deals with Saudis, 16 of whom hijacked airplanes and killed thousands of Americans.

Then there's the issue of gay rights and same-sex marriage. The Republican Party does not condone or accept homosexuality, and if anyone tells you it does, they simply want money or are thinking wishfully. That doesn't mean individual Republican politicians haven't done anything nice for the community—politicians will do anything to benefit themselves, even pander to those their party despises. But today they made their stance clear. This debate is not about gay marriage, but about putting a big "NO" stamp on the heads of gays and lesbians nationally. I've said it before, I'll say it again. We were moving forward and now they want to bat us down with the U.S. Constitution.

We are in a social civil war right now, one being led by the religious right—and the Republican Party is not only a part of that but entwined and synonymous with it. And in a war there are three options: this side, that side, or neutral. You can't change the enemy by becoming them. The Republican Party will never change its stance on certain issues because (a) it doesn't want to, (b) its major contributors don't want it to, and (c) God's not coming back anytime soon to tell them how ridiculously wrong they are—and He's the only one these rich white men (and women) will listen to. Even if he did come back and try to set them straight, they'd keep it silenced. God would be a Libertarian, and they wouldn't like that. They'd reinstate crucifixions, Mel Gibson would have real footage for his sequel, *The Passion of the Bush*, and all would be well in their eyes.

I once had a tolerance level for gay Republicans. But no longer. There comes a time when you leave a place, an organization, a job, a church, a family because it has turned against you so many times and shows no signs of changing. They're called toxic relationships. Republicans who are gay are in a toxic relationship with their party, and if the party had its druthers, the toxicity would be fatal.

I'm not saying Democrats are better. Clinton signed the federal Defense of Marriage Act and enacted the failed, flawed, and generally wretched "don't ask, don't tell" policy for the military. And not one of the major Democratic presidential candidates took Bush to task directly over his suggesting gay marriage be banned by constitutional amendment. Where are Kerry and Edwards today? Silent. They haven't shut up for weeks on the campaign trail, but they're not in any hurry to make a statement this morning.

While the Democratic Party has historically been better toward gays and lesbians, if it were really gung ho on civil rights, this marriage issue would have been solved a long time ago and other equal protection legislation would have been enacted. No, they've dragged their feet. They are what you call in war an ally, certainly. They have an agenda, one that may not always include your benefit, but they will come to your aide to some degree and can be powerful. And we need allies.

I wrote an editorial recently about the president making me choose sides and dividing me from the ranks of those who wanted compromise. Well, thanks again, Mr. President. Now, you've divided me within my own ranks. You've taken my tolerance of those with different views—those who choose to be gay Republicans and would vote again for you—and turned it into disgust. Any gay person who would vote for George W. Bush in 2004 has serious problems when it comes to reality. It's sad that it's come to that. But it has, through Bush's own doing. The question is, Will gays and lesbians see that clearly? Or will they stand on some ghost of what they think their party stands for, some rose-colored view of what it might have been instead of the right-wing, ultraconservative, corporate-kissing, warmongering entity it has plainly become?

The president finally drew the national battle lines with his persistent talk of "protecting" marriage and launched his scud missile on February 24, 2004. So now the lines have been drawn. If you're gay, there's only one obvious side.

No, you say? How dare I? Well, you're right. You can be gay and still wish to be a Republican and reelect Bush. Everyone's entitled to vote their conscience. But remember, if you do, there is no more gray area: You betray every gay and lesbian person out there, because you say you're trying to work from within while that same entity you're trying to change is busy insulting, demeaning, degrading, segregating, and ultimately humiliating your people on the federal level. They have opened the door for all who would oppose us to have a voice and be taken seriously. They have let the lunatics run the asylum.

There's a time to stay. And a time to leave. It's time to show the Republicans they've gone too far. It's time to unite against this new platform of divisiveness and war, the politics of social separation through fear and the heavy-handedness of one religion. It's time to tell the Republicans no matter what their moderates say, what their pundits promote, we've seen through it and seen them for who they are. And we no longer wish to be part of that and will do all we can to stop it. It's time gays and lesbians realize they are gay *first* and Republican, Democrat, independent, whatever, second. When you are being attacked, you protect yourself from the enemy. On the front line. Not from within.

Yes, that's a departure for me. I don't believe in being "gay" first. I believe in being human. And that's what makes this even harder. You see, we *are* human, whether they like it or not, and *all* humans are entitled to certain inalienable rights. But since POTUS doesn't read the papers, he's probably not bothered with the Constitution either.

You Only Have One

My mother left December 29, 2003. Now, some say she died, but they weren't there—I was. She just left. Her body had grown too weak to house her spirit, her energy, her will to do more. The spirit held on and on and on. But it left her body.

She had been in a nursing home since July 29, 2003. Each and every day she spoke of when she'd return home. She had COPD, the fourth-biggest killer in the United States. Most people don't even know what it is. In an era of diseases with initials, AIDS seems to have the monopoly. COPD is an umbrella condition, like AIDS. It is chronic obstructive pulmonary disease. Asthma, chronic bronchitis, emphysema, and congestive heart failure fall under this umbrella. Mom had them all. One day she could walk, the next day she couldn't. She grew too weak, wasn't getting enough air.

But her brain certainly got oxygen, and she never rested. I know because I was there, through it all. In fact, I've been there, through it all, my entire life. I've always been close to my mother. I was there for her, as she was always there for me. Even more so since my father died December 28, 1987. Yes, they died exactly 15 years and one day apart.

After the funeral everyone began telling me their stories. Fans of my radio show, e-mailers, friends, other people at the home, nurses——each of them had a story about someone who took care of their mother like I did mine. And each time the person in the story, the caregiver, was a son, a gay son.

I want to make a blanket statement here, one that became so clear to me in recent years: Gay men love their mothers more. But I can't say that, right? Since I've never been a straight man with a mother. But from all the conclusive evidence I've seen, for some reason we are closer to our mothers than our nongay male counterparts.

I've sat and wondered why we are. Maybe, if the mother is accepting, we feel a debt, a duty to her because we grew up hearing how parents don't have to accept us for who we are. I would say that's true, but no parent has to accept their child's lifestyle, really.

You know, as I sit trying to analyze it, to editorialize, to make it clear, I realize suddenly I don't want to be fair, I don't want to be clear, I don't want to be balanced. *Of course* gay men love their mothers more. We speak their language. We have a bond that nongay children could never have with them. The facades are stripped down; our most personal, human side of us is exposed——and they love us right back. The gender boundaries are gone.

When my mother was in the nursing home she wouldn't let a male nurse change her, but she'd let me. She wouldn't let a male nurse take her to the bathroom or shower her, but she'd let me. Why? Because our love was unconditional and unpretentious.

Who cares if it's a stereotype that gay men bond more with our mothers? I for one am proud of that. And as I sit here, in the devastation caused by her death, I realize I will miss that bond even more than the one I had with my late husband. Why? Because you only get one mom. There may be another man out there to love me, as my friends keep telling me, but there was only one Rose Marie Tremblay Bouley.

For those of us lucky enough to be close to our mothers, they provide a sense of home for us, of stability. No matter what happens in the crazy gay world of ours, we can always count on them for advice, to drive us crazy, to go shopping with, to remind us why we shouldn't have dated that guy-or to reach out to us when they need a hand. They are not just our moms but our confidants. The bravado of straighthood doesn't drive a wedge between us. There is no bravado between gay men and their mothers.

Now, I know lesbians love their moms too. There was a lesbian couple taking care of one of their moms at the home. In fact, I saw their faces right before walking into the room as Mom breathed her last. They were in the hall, coaching their mom to walk a few more steps. But it's odd-I watched day after day, and the mom treated the lesbian daughter much more like a straight son. It was funny to me.

In any event, I still contend gay men get an extra bonus, an extra something between them and their moms, especially as they grow older. It's odd that one of the insults pointed toward gay men has historically been to be called a "mama's boy." Well, I'm one, and I couldn't be happier. I got to be a part of an extraordinary life. I learned lessons in courage and hope from my mother that kept me strong as I faced life as an out gay male. I learned about perseverance through adversity; I gained perspective about mortality; I saw that raising me wasn't always the easiest of things but that taking care of someone, including the mother caring for the son and vice versa, brings its own rewards. I learned no event is special unless you make a pan of lasagna, and I learned that even when your parent falls ill and is weak, you can still get so much strength from them.

Yes, I was close to my mother. Yes, many, many gay men are. Some keep that more closeted than their sexuality. Some get embarrassed. Not me. Every holiday, every party, every weekend, my little 4-foot-9 mom was here, at my house, both when Andrew was alive and after. She loved all her "boys" and loved how they took care of her and came to see her when she fell ill. My mother was a matriarchal figure not only to me but to many of my gay male friends. Everybody loved Rose. Everybody still does.

I know gay men love their mothers more by the length of time it takes for us to grieve their loss, by the sadness it causes when they leave. Of all the parts about being gay, it may be the one character trait for which I am most grateful. I can't imagine not really knowing my mom, really understanding her. I can't imagine not taking time each day to speak to her and see her. I can't imagine what it's going to be like now that I can't.

If your mother is still here, love her. Tell her. Strengthen or rebuild that bond that only a gay son and his mom can have. It's one of the most precious gifts being gay can bring. Cherish it like the gold it is. And remember, there's only one.